THE SCIENCE OF MIND MANAGEMENT

THE SCIENCE OF MIND MANAGEMENT

SWAMI
MUKUNDANANDA

First published by Westland Publications Private Limited in 2020

1st Floor, A Block, East Wing, Plot No. 40, SP Infocity, Dr MGR Salai, Perungudi, Kandanchavadi, Chennai 600096

ISBN: 9789389648447

10 9 8 7 6 5 4 3 2 1

Typeset by Jojy Philip, New Delhi - 110015
Printed at Thomson Press (India) Ltd.

CONTENTS

DEDICATION

This book is dedicated to my Spiritual Master, Jagadguru Shree Kripalu-ji Maharaj, the embodiment of divine love and grace, who munificently revealed the most sublime spiritual knowledge for the welfare of humankind.

As the Supreme Jagadguru of this age, he repeatedly taught the importance of purifying the mind. He emphasised that 'it is the mind alone which is the cause of bondage and liberation'. For its cleansing and sublimation, he revealed many powerful techniques, including roop dhyan meditation, reflection, contemplation, selfless devotion, surrender, and the practice of karm yog in our personal sadhana.

I am eternally indebted to him for bestowing upon me his divine wisdom, and for inspiring me to consecrate my life to its propagation. I pray with all my heart that he will be pleased with my humble endeavour to present the perennial Vedic knowledge in a modern context.

INTRODUCTION

As we strive to upgrade the quality of our life's experiences, we begin to realise the importance of the mind. It creates our perceptions of happiness and distress. If it goes astray, it robs our inner joy, dragging us into a cesspool of miserable thoughts and feelings. But if effectively trained, the mind becomes our biggest resource for optimism, contentment, determination, and joyfulness. That is why the Vedic scriptures have rightly called it the cause of both bondage and liberation.

The mind is like a fertile field. If you cultivate it well, it blossoms with attractive plants and beautiful flowers. But if neglected, the outcome is terrible: wild weeds and thorny shrubs!

Likewise, the mind is replete with infinite potential. As gardeners of the mind, we must ensure its productivity. Our sovereign duty in life is to carefully tend to our mind to make it bloom with sublime thoughts and noble emotions.

We can fulfil this duty by learning about the science of mind management, one of the most useful skills we can learn in life.

The successful distinguish themselves by their ability to marshal their mental resources. They choose their thoughts judiciously to be ever happy and inspired. As masters of their mind, they prefer to focus their thoughts and energy upon their goals, promptly discarding negative emotions as useless baggage. They know how to tap into the fountain source of inspiration that lies within. Thus, they march forth as more effective human beings.

In contrast are those who remain slaves of their emotions. Unable to control their ideas and feelings, they become victims of the environment. They feel that the key to happiness lies in external factors. To be happy, they desperately need others to behave differently and for situations to change. Hence, they become obsessed with battling circumstances in their life.

Wouldn't it have been easier if they had prioritised improving their own mind? Had they done that, they would have found an infallible and trustworthy friend within themselves. That's why even a little time dedicated to acquiring the technology for mind management reaps rich dividends, enriching your life forever.

The very fact that you are devoting your precious time to read this book implies that you recognise the value of training the mind. In this book, you will discover powerful techniques for transforming your life, such as chintan (contemplation), self-affirmation, visualisation, yoga of the intellect, roop dhyan meditation, and śharaṇāgati (surrender to the Supreme), among others.

I learned these secrets from Jagadguru Shree Kripalu-ji Maharaj, who was the fifth original Jagadguru of Indian history. He personally coached me for twenty-five beautiful years in the practical application of these teachings to my life. What I gained from this indescribable experience is beyond words. Suffice it to say that the practice bestowed an inestimable treasure of love, knowledge, and bliss that only keeps growing each day

Maharaj-ji entrusted me with the key task of sharing the divine knowledge I have received from him. This has been my life's mission for over three decades now. With that goal, I extensively studied ancient Vedic texts and the scriptures of all the major Eastern and Western religious traditions of the world. Further, I delved into the teachings of scores of other great saints in Indian history—Kabir, Tulsidas, Narsi Mehta, Tukaram, Meerabai, Guru Nanak, Ekanath, Soordas, and many more. To highlight the universality of the principles that I teach, these saints and scriptures have been extensively quoted in this book. Additionally, sayings of illustrious personalities in history, who reached the same conclusions from their experience, are also included in this book.

The principles described herein are explained with systematic logic, to show their rationality and reasoning. Finally, since this is a book on the practical application of spirituality, I have also given plenty of real-life instances and stories to help convey the ideas dramatically and vividly.

It is always a good idea to understand genuine knowledge through a mix of logic, stories, examples, and scriptural quotations—as they not only help to convince us but also to retain and internalise the teachings.

During the last thirty years, I have shared these principles with millions of people and seen them benefit from them.

With the blessings of the Supreme Lord, may the book truly enrich your life and help you experience the fountain of joy, inspiration, and love within.

THE NEED FOR MIND MANAGEMENT

We all wish to enhance the quality of our life to feel joyful and happy. We desire to think noble and sublime thoughts. We wish to do productive work that makes a difference in the world. In short, we all seek to be better human beings. An auto-script embedded within our soul inspires us to be more perfect, more godlike.

Yet, not everyone achieves their cherished goals. While a few lead inspired lives with noble values, and find deep satisfaction in their work and relationships, the vast majority stumble along the journey of life, tripping repeatedly over anger, greed, tension, and anxiety. No matter how much they struggle, they seem to attract misery and failure. And even if they do succeed externally, their hearts stay dejected and happiness eludes them.

Why is reality so different from our dreams and aspirations? It is not money, power, fame, or an affluent upbringing that determines the quality of our life. There are many successful people who had very little of these external resources, and yet they achieved happiness, productivity, and fulfilment. There are also innumerable others who had all these but still could not lift themselves from wretchedness. Where did they go wrong?

The Key to Happiness and Success

An example of an inspired individual was Helen Keller, a renowned philanthropist of the last century. When she was only nineteen months old, a severe infection made her deaf and blind. Consequently, she could not learn to speak and often threw tantrums to communicate her frustration to her family.

When Helen Keller was seven years old, her parents found a special needs school and a willing teacher in Anne Sullivan. Partially blind herself, Anne first tried teaching language to little Helen by signing letters onto the child's hand. Helen did not immediately respond, but the patient teacher was determined to find a way to communicate with the young girl.

One day, Anne placed Helen's hand under a waterspout. With cool water running over one hand, Anne wrote the letters 'w-a-t-e-r' on Helen's other hand. Suddenly, something clicked within Helen. For the first time in her life she understood that external objects had names. She was so excited that she eagerly begged to learn more names. By nightfall, she had learned the names of thirty more objects.

Helen proceeded to enthusiastically learn the signs for people and things in her outside world. She picked up the Braille system for the blind. Soon, she started grasping abstract ideas like the meaning of the word 'love'. As this door opened new ways to understand the world, she devoted herself to learning all she could. She began to read classical books and books of knowledge like other students of her age.

As a young adult, Helen became determined to join Harvard University, although her parents and friends were not so encouraging. Helen persevered, passed the required tests, and was accepted at Radcliffe College, the women's college associated with Harvard. She graduated with academic honours, despite the fact that she was deaf, blind, and unable to speak.

Helen now wanted to learn to speak like others around her. She was guided to touch the face, mouth, and throat of Anne Sullivan while her teacher was speaking, and astoundingly Helen responded to this kinaesthetic experience by producing the sounds of speech herself. Helen learned to speak well enough to give lectures that, over time, inspired normal, deaf, and blind people everywhere. In her later years, Helen became a philanthropist seeking ways to fund the education of others. She lived till the ripe age of eighty-seven.

Here are a couple of her famous quotations to savour:

> When one door of happiness closes, another opens; but often we look so long at the closed door that we do not see the one which has been opened for us.
>
> Life is exciting business, and most exciting when it is lived for others.

Contrast Helen Keller with others whose outer circumstances were exceptionally favourable, yet they failed miserably.

One such person was Elvis Presley, an icon of the rock and roll generation. He was handsome, wealthy, a movie actor, possessed a golden voice, and often called 'The King of Rock and Roll'. Yet, he was wretchedly unhappy, and often used a round of drugs to gear up for a musical performance followed by another round to calm him down after the performance.

Elvis Presley gorged on drugs, sex, and songs that possibly thrilled his fans more than him. Though externally he was so successful, yet internally he was nearly bankrupt. He died prematurely at the age of forty-two with heart complications, other serious health problems, and a long-time addiction to drugs.

The singer once lamented:

Truth is like the sun. You can shut it out for a while but it ain't going away.

How different were these two luminaries! What did Helen Keller have that enabled her to succeed beyond imagination, despite possessing only three of the normal five human senses? And what did Elvis Presley not have that he failed so miserably in his personal life, although he lacked neither wealth, fame, nor talent? The key difference lay in the state of their mind.

The Mind–Our Best Friend and Worst Enemy

Our mind is the single-most important factor that determines the quality of our life. Successfully controlled, it becomes our best ally, but if allowed to run wild, it steals our inner peace and undermines all our productive endeavours.

The Vedic scriptures inform us:

uddhared ātmanātmānaṁ nātmānam avasādayet
ātmaiva hyātmano bandhur ātmaiva ripur ātmanaḥ

(Bhagavad Gita 6.5)

'Elevate yourself through the power of your mind, and not degrade yourself, for the mind can be the greatest assistant of the self, and also its vilest enemy.'

What is this mind? It is a subtle machine fitted within us by God. While the body is the external machinery, the mind is the internal one. Its function is to generate thoughts, and it profusely engages in this activity throughout the waking state. It continues to work even when we dream. Only in deep sleep does the mind rest. This is why, when people wake up from slumber, they say:

sukhamahamasvāpsam 'I slept very peacefully.'
na kiñchimahamavediśham 'I did not experience anything.'

During deep sleep, the mind is at rest, and you experience blissful peace. At all other times, it stays active and creates thoughts incessantly.

We experience both happiness and distress because of the state of our mind. Let us say that someone is in a miserable mood. You tell her something that generates a happy thought in her, and she smiles in glee. Next, presume another person is in a good mood. You convey bad news to him, which creates a miserable thought, and he instantly grimaces in despair. Both the experiences of glee and despair are results of the state of the mind.

Learn to cultivate a cheerful mind, and you will experience heavenly bliss even in the midst of the most hellish circumstances. On the other hand, if we harbour a miserable mind, we will suffer the torments of hell even if we are surrounded by heavenly luxury. British poet and philosopher, John Milton, described this perfectly in *Paradise Lost*:

> The mind is a place of its own, and in itself can make heaven out of hell and hell out of heaven.

We dissipate a large portion of our energy in combating external enemies whom we perceive as potentially harmful to us. But the Vedic scriptures say the biggest foes such as lust, anger, greed, envy, and illusion reside in our own mind. These internal adversaries are even more pernicious than the outer ones. External opponents may injure us for a while, but the demons within have the ability to make every moment a living hell. For example, when our mind harbours animosity, the negative thoughts generated do more damage than the object of our hatred. Hence, it has been wisely said: 'Resentment is like drinking poison and hoping that the other person dies.' The poison referred to is the negativity we harbour within.

The Buddha expressed this truth vividly:

> I have been insulted! I have been hurt! I have been beaten! I have been robbed! Misery does not cease in those who harbour such thoughts.
>
> I have been insulted! I have been hurt! I have been beaten! I have been robbed! Anger ceases in those who do not harbour such thoughts. (Dhammapada 1.3)

If someone accidentally throws a stone at us, it may hurt for a few minutes, but by the next day, we would probably have forgotten about it. However, if someone says something unpleasant, it can agitate us for years. On the other hand, if we can get rid of such thoughts, we will experience sublime peace. Given the role of thoughts in bestowing hellish misery or celestial joy, it becomes important that we understand their power.

The Nature of Thoughts

What are thoughts? They are subtle bundles of energy created in the factory of the mind. The atmosphere around us is full of energy waves that are invisible to the naked eye. If we take a radio set and rotate the channel tuner, broadcasting stations appear in quick succession to reveal their existence. Radio waves are there though we cannot see them. Similarly, thoughts too are subtle waves generated by the mind.

Our thoughts impact us in multiple ways. Our body reacts to every thought we have, literally even chiselling our physical appearance. This is why we look at someone and remark, 'Stay away from him. He seems to be a very angry guy.' Or we look at another and say, 'She seems like a very simple person. We can rely on her.' In either case, the thoughts within sculpted the person's external looks.

Secondly, thoughts fructify into actions. They are the internal roots from which all actions spring. This is based on a simple principle: good thoughts fructify into good actions and bad thoughts fructify into bad actions. Those who dedicate their lives to the service of humankind do not land there by accident. For years, they cultivated compassionate and noble thoughts in their mind, until the energy of those accumulated thoughts blossomed into inspiring acts of sacrifice and service.

Similarly, those who commit theft and murder naively blame circumstances for their sins. If we were to delve deeper, we would discover that they harboured sinful thoughts in their mind, and circumstances literally aligned themselves to fulfil their desires.

If we wish to draw more favourable circumstances in our life, let's begin by improving our thoughts. Without understanding this cause-and-effect relationship, we put the cart before the horse when we struggle to discard bad actions from our personality without changing the underlying thoughts.

Like diligent horticulturists, we must carefully weed out all kinds of negative thoughts that sprout, such as anger, greed, hatred, envy, illusion, fear, and anxiety, from the orchard of our mind. When we strive to improve the state of our mind, we then realise the import of the Vedic injunction:

mana eva manuṣhyāṇāṁ kāraṇaṁ bandha mokṣhayoḥ
(*Pañchadaśhī*)

'The mind is the cause of bondage and the mind is the cause of liberation.'

The Buddha stated the same principle in different words:

> Suffering follows an evil thought as the wheels of a cart follow the oxen that draws it. Joy follows a pure thought like a shadow that never leaves. (Dhammapada 1.1)

The level of our consciousness is tied to our mind. Veritably, we are what our mind is. This is why the wise sages said:

bhūla na jānā isa nuskhe ko, lābh anek uṭhāoge
jaisā mana ko banā sakoge, vaise hī bana jāoge

'Do not forget these golden words; you will derive great benefit from them. The extent to which you uplift or degrade your mind, so your soul will be uplifted or degraded accordingly.'

The Mind-Body Connection

We have seen how thoughts impact both our physical appearance and our actions. You may be surprised to learn that thoughts even impact our health. The *Yog Vāsiṣhṭh*, an ancient scripture, tells a revealing story about the mind-body connection.

Lord Ram once undertook a tour of His kingdom, to personally observe the condition of His people. He was dismayed to see them suffering from disease. Returning to His palace, He asked His preceptor, Maharshi Vasishth, 'Guru-ji, what is the cause of disease?'

Guru Vasishth replied, 'Ram, disease begins in the mind. When we harbour poisonous thoughts, the Manomaya kośh (mental sheath) gets disturbed. This agitates the Prāṇamaya kośh (vital energy sheath). That disturbance manifests in the Annamaya kośh (physical body) as disease.'

This is, of course, a very simplistic explanation, for we all know that diseases can have innumerable causes. Ayurveda, too, talks of two kinds of diseases—*doṣhaj* and *karmaj*. Doṣhaj diseases are reactions to bad karmas or actions from our past lives, while karmaj diseases are a consequence of defective habits of eating, sleeping, thinking, working, etc. in the present life. Behind both are negative thoughts that result in harmful habits and immoral actions.

In the last few decades, modern medical science has begun acknowledging the mind-body connection. A powerful example of this is the placebo effect. A placebo is a harmless substance, like a sugar pill, given to patients instead of prescription drugs. However, patients are told they are being given medicine for their ailment. The consequence of consuming the placebo is that patients mentally believe they will now get well, and their thoughts induce them to recuperate, even without taking actual medicine! One such study on the use of placebos was conducted by Dr Stewart Wolf in the 1950s.

Dr Wolf conducted research on pregnant women who have a natural tendency to vomit in the first few months of pregnancy. When they would complain to Dr Wolf of symptoms of vomiting, he would give them Ipecac, a drug that induces vomiting. Ipecac is often kept in laboratories as a safeguard. If anyone accidentally swallows poison and needs to vomit it out, Ipecac is administered to induce the vomit. When Dr Wolf administered the drug to the pregnant women, as expected, the symptoms of vomiting were exacerbated. He would then tell them, 'Do not worry. I have a wonder drug that has just been launched. It has been tested on thousands of patients and found to bring about miraculous suppression of the vomiting tendency. I will administer it to you now.'

Then he would give them the same Ipecac that had earlier aggravated their urge to vomit. But this time, the symptoms of vomiting would disappear for the night. The next morning, the tendency to vomit would again return.

What was the reason for the cure, even though it was the very drug that induces vomiting? It was the placebo effect. The patients' mind told them that they should feel better, and their bodies responded to their thoughts.

'Placebo effect' can sometimes have a demeaning connotation and is often not well-received by patients. If you tell people they got cured by the placebo effect, they are likely to say, 'You mean it was all in my mind?' As a result, Herbert Benson and Richard Friedman coined the term, 'remembered wellness'. It is the phenomenon in which the subconscious mind remembers the state of wellness and replicates it in the present.

The phenomenon of 'remembered wellness' commonly occurs when patients visit their family physician. The doctor says, 'Show me your symptoms,' and patients find that their symptoms have disappeared. The mere fact that they are meeting the doctor tells their subconscious mind that they will now get well. Consequently, 'remembered wellness' takes place and healing occurs.

The reverse of this is 'remembered illness', a common example of which is white collar hypertension. Patients may have perfect blood pressure at home, but when they visit the doctor, they find it has increased. What is the reason for this? In their minds, they think that since they are visiting the hospital, they must be unwell. They recall a previous state of illness, and the body responds to their thoughts by increasing the blood pressure. This is a perfect example of the mind making the body sick.

These examples demonstrate how illness is caused not only by viruses and bacteria but also by the negativities the mind harbours. Thus, mere physical cure of a medical condition is not enough. True health requires managing the mind along with taking care of the body. In fact, the World Health Organization (WHO) defines health as: 'The state of complete physical, mental, and social well-being, and not merely the absence of disease or infirmity.'

Unfortunately, in the commotion of life, we often put mind management on the backseat, while we passionately pursue external success, not realising that inner victories are the real basis for outer accomplishments. Let us, therefore, gain a better perspective on what goes on within us.

The Inner and Outer Worlds

The world we encounter is of two kinds. The first is the external world made of earth, water, fire, air, and space. Since it is created by God, the Master Architect and Designer, it is perfect—just like Him. The Vedas go to the extent of saying that God Himself becomes the world:

yathorṇa-nābhiḥ sṛijate gṛihṇate cha,
yathā pṛithivyām oṣhadhayaḥ sambhavanti
yathā sataḥ puruṣhāt keśha-lomāni
tathākṣharāt sambhavatīha viśhvam

(*Muṇḍakopaniṣhad* 1.1.7)

'As the spider extracts its web from its own body, and reabsorbs it later, similarly at the time of creation, God too manifests the world from within His own being, and then absorbs it back into Himself at the time of dissolution.' In other words, the world is an inseparable part of God.

Again, the Vedas state:

īśhāvāsyam idam sarvaṁ yat kiñcha jagatyāṁ jagat
(*Īśhopaniṣhad* verse 1)

'The entire world and everything in it is the veritable form of God.'

Since the Creator is perfect and complete, the world is also perfect and complete. This external world was created to sustain the physical body. **Apart from the gross external world, there is also a subtle inner world** that each of us creates in our own mind. This is the realm of our desires, attachments, and aversions, due to our *sanskārs* or accumulated tendencies of endless lifetimes. While the external world is the same for all, everyone's inner world is different and unique.

Between these two worlds, the inner one is far more compelling. Agitation by physical objects is possible only as long as desires for them are present in the mind. If these desires are vanquished from within, then external objects no longer hold sway over us. In the Ramayan, Lord Ram said of his younger brother, Bharat:

bharatahi hoi na rājamadu bidhi hari hara pada pāi

'What to speak of becoming proud by ascending the throne of Ayodhya? Bharat can never develop pride even if he ascends the throne of Brahma, Shankar, or Vishnu.' The reason for Ram's confidence in the infallibility of Bharat was that his inner world was clean and pure. Bharat had reached a state where his mind was free from the everyday material sentiments of anger, desire, jealousy, greed, and lust. As a result, he could never be swayed by the lure of power in the outer world.

Lord Shiv emphasised the same maxim:

umā je rāma charaṇa rata vigata kāma mada krodha,
nija prabhumaya dekhahiñ jagata kehi sana karahiñ birodha

(Ramayan)

'O Parvati, those noble souls who free themselves from desire, pride, and anger see the world as the form of their beloved Lord. Towards whom can they be inimical?'

Hence, all saints who succeeded in purifying their inner world experienced the external world as the veritable form of God.

Thus, the situations in the external world cannot be the cause of our strife. Rather, it is the other way around—inner thoughts bring external circumstances onto us—as will be explained in the next section.

Thought by Thought, We Forge Our Destiny

When we encounter difficulties, we tend to hold the outer world responsible for our woes. But, circumstances do not come by the throw of a dice. The world is governed not by chaos, but by eternal principles. And although it may not seem so to us, God has made this world perfectly to enable our purification.

Consider the example of Ramdutt, who is always annoyed to no end with the irascible behaviour of Vishnudutt, his obnoxious neighbour. To get away from him, Ramdutt finally moves to another neighbourhood only to find that his new neighbour is no better than Vishnudutt. The experience repeats itself over and over again. Every time he moves, he encounters an equally obnoxious neighbour.

Eventually, Ramdutt decides to see the situation positively and begins using it as an opportunity to develop his own tolerance and patience, the very two virtues in which he is deficient. He realises that circumstances in his life have schemed for that very purpose. When he finally masters equipoise despite the worst behaviour of his neighbour, he suddenly finds the situation changing. Lo, behold! Wonderful citizens begin moving into his neighbourhood.

In this manner, the material energy, maya, arranges for the salvation of our soul. **Circumstances come in our life for a purpose, and they remain until the purpose is served.** When we have learned the lessons intended for us, the environment naturally changes and leads to a new set of situations that carry within them another lesson.

This is a simple explanation of our life circumstances. Everyone is a mixture of virtues and frailties, just as situations are a myriad web of intricate constraints and opportunities. It is naïve to think that we understand the precise reason for any particular situation in our life. Many circumstances are the result of our karmas or past actions either in the present lifetime or in prior ones. It's literally time for stocktaking. If we had sinned grievously in the past, painful situations come as punishment. They teach us that actions have consequences and that we should not sin again.

At other times, God merely supplies us a rope to hang ourselves with, the situations providing ample opportunities to indulge in our most debased desire. Lessons follow much later through ill-health, penury and infamy, among others. The so-called 'Law of Attraction,' now so glibly touted in the world is actually a very incomplete and inaccurate representation of reality.[1] Nevertheless, the link between our inner desires, in the past or the present, and the circumstances in our life always exists.

People rarely understand this cause-and-effect chain and keep fighting with circumstances, blaming situations for all their miseries and feeling woefully victimised by them. The Law of Karma is very just; it takes into account our actions from all the past lifetimes. Where we are in life today is the result of our thoughts and actions in the past. Our thoughts today decide where we will be in life tomorrow. Rather than play the blame game or curse Lady Luck, we must focus on improving ourselves. The more we win our inner battles, the more we will find external success knocking at our door. It's quite simple—thought by thought, we forge our destiny.

---

[1] The 'Law of Attraction' states that merely by thinking of wealth and success, we can attract these in our lives. This is a very simplistic understanding, for thoughts need to be followed by massive effort. Also, the circumstances in our life cannot be explained from a simple one-to-one mapping with our present thoughts. There are many other factors as well that determine what happens to us, such as our past karmas, the efforts of others, the karmas of all the souls in that place, the will of God, etc.

Let's look at a young lady who leads a mediocre existence but cherishes a life full of purpose and value. She nurtures thoughts of pleasing God through loving service to society. The sublime thoughts of kind-heartedness and empathy seize her consciousness so strongly that she is filled with passion for making a difference in the lives of people. In a short while, opportunity knocks on her door to become an entrepreneur. She now finds herself pioneering a new cottage industry that trains hundreds of village women in self-employment. People marvel at her success, and the ignorant say that she simply got lucky. But the wise smile, knowing that she got what she merited.

This perfect universe is not a game of roulette where any crackpot can win the jackpot! A Taoist saying captures this perfectly: 'The snowflakes fall slowly to the ground; each flake to its proper place'. There are eternal laws that govern the world, and the Law of Karma is one of them. When the lady deserved it, the Universe provided her with just the right opportunity to serve according to her heart's desire. She made her life a success, and so can we, if we marshal our resources well.

According to the Vedas, God created the world through His material energy, maya. All the gross and subtle elements of the world have evolved from this material energy. Since it is God's shakti or energy, maya always acts in His service, and works to fulfil His divine will. Thus, it orchestrates situations in the world for the gradual elevation of the soul, continually pushing us to move from our present state to perfection.

You would have noticed that nothing in life and in this world is constant. We are incessantly pushed to grow and evolve. As soon as we learn one lesson, the next one is presented to us. Life is like a book that is constantly teaching us lessons. Having come in this world, improve we must. Be open to this learning. Let this world not become the 'University of Hard Knocks', where we are forced to progress the hard way—through difficult experiences. The wise do not waste their energy in cursing circumstances. They quickly learn the lessons inherent in the situation, and progress rapidly forward on the journey of internal growth and development.

Leverage the Resources God Has Blessed Us With

After reading the success story in the previous section, we may wonder if we have what it takes to succeed likewise. We do, but instead of realising the importance of what we have, we remain focused on what we lack. Let me tell you the story of a beggar I once met.

It was over two decades ago in a little town called Aska, in the state of Odisha in Eastern India. I was walking in the morning by myself. As I approached a bridge, I saw a mendicant standing atop the railing, gathering courage to plunge into the river below. It was obvious that he was about to give up his life.

I screamed, 'What are you doing? Please stop!'

Startled, he looked at me and hesitated. He jumped back onto the road, and I ran to grab his arm.

'Why were you considering such a cowardly act?' I chided him. 'Don't you know that if you had committed suicide, you would have to become a ghost in your next life? As punishment for

rejecting your physical body, you would then not possess a gross body in your next life; you would have to live as a ghost with just a subtle body. That would be a very painful existence because you would have material desires, but no way of fulfilling them.'

Hearing about the consequences of suicide made him change his mind. He began sharing with me the pain he was harbouring within. 'God has given me nothing,' he whined. 'I have only poverty and misery to look forward to in life.'

'If I give you 50 lakh rupees (nearly $75,000), will you become positive about your future?' I asked him.

'Of course I will,' he retorted.

'Okay, but in exchange I will need something from you—you will have to give me your two eyes.'

'What? Do you expect me to be blind? I cannot give you my eyes.'

'That means your eyes are more valuable than 50 lakh rupees. This is why you are not willing to part with them for that sum of money. You were saying that God has given you nothing. Count your eyes as the first grace of God.'

'Okay,' I continued, 'I am willing to offer you another deal. Take 25 lakh rupees (nearly $37,500) and give me your two arms.'

'Absolutely not! I would rather have my arms than your 25 lakh rupees.'

'That means your arms are more valuable than 25 lakh rupees. Count another grace of God. Will you give me your two legs, if I offer you 15 lakh rupees (nearly $22,500)?'

In this way, I kept assigning a value to his different body parts, in accordance with his perception.

'Look,' I said, 'You have over one crore rupees (almost $150,000) right here in your body. The problem is that, though you have received so much from God, you have not realised the value of His gifts.'

Like that mendicant, we too tend to undervalue the graces we have received from the benevolent Lord. All of us are blessed with two wonderful eyes, each fitted with 125 million photoreceptors for converting light into electric signals. They help us see the colours of the rainbow, the crimson sky of the setting sun, the plumes of the peacock, the dewdrops on the lotus leaf, and the flight of an eagle. Isn't that an exceptional grace that we should be delighted about?

Similarly, we often take the gift of hearing for granted. Imagine what life would be like if we couldn't hear the sounds in our environment? Fortunately, we are blessed with two ears, each fitted with 30,000 fibres, with which we hear sounds in a wide audio spectrum, ranging from 20 Hz to 20,000 Hz, including leaves rustling in the wind, ocean waves hitting the rocks, acoustics of a theatrical symphony, and spasmodic thuds of a woodpecker against a tree trunk. Isn't it an invaluable gift for which we ought to be more grateful?

Again, we are blessed with a tongue that in conjunction with a sound box can create words to heal, console, uplift, entertain, cheer, and educate. How fortunate for us!

Our brain is fitted with a 100 billion neurons that combine to make trillions of circuits. This gives us the ability to appreciate the perspicacity of Upanishadic knowledge, the aesthetics of Shakespeare's plays, the logic of a computer software programme, the ethical ramifications of a situation, and the legality of our actions.

Our blood flows through nearly 100,000 kilometres of arteries and capillaries to deliver oxygen and nutrients to almost 40 trillion cells in our body. To drive the blood, the heart beats a hundred thousand times in a single day and 36 million times in a year. How miraculous!

We have a musculoskeletal system with 650 muscles, 206 bones, and 11 kilometres of nerve fibre, all synchronised to work at our command. They enable us to climb mountain peaks, run down valleys, dive into lakes. and swim across rivers. What a blessing!

The organs in our body perform such complex functions that if these activities were to be replicated by machines, it would require a factory the size of a warehouse. It is obvious that we are beneficiaries of abundant grace!

The list of our individual assets—physical and mental—can run into scores of pages. Yet, despite all the graces bestowed upon us, why is it that some people manage their resources so well that they move from accomplishment to accomplishment, while others squander them and stagger from failure to failure?

Once again, the answer lies in the state of the mind. The successful distinguish themselves from failures by their attitude which is the ability to manage their own inner state.

We have seen how the quality of our life—including joy, health, circumstances, and productivity at work—depends upon our state of mind. This book on the science of managing the mind is thus a powerful means of enriching ourselves. Let us understand this science and apply it in our daily life.

SUMMARY OF THE MAIN POINTS

- Our mind has the potential of becoming our best friend or worst enemy. A controlled mind is our best friend while an uncontrolled mind is our worst enemy.
- The mind is a subtle machine within us that incessantly creates thoughts.
- Thoughts are little bundles of energy that impact us in multiple ways and affect our appearance, health, experience of happiness, and much more.
- Most importantly, thoughts fructify into actions. If we wish to improve our actions, we must begin by improving the thoughts we harbour within ourselves.
- Thought by thought, we forge our destiny. When we cultivate noble and sublime thoughts in our mind, we naturally draw favourable circumstances in our life.
- The external world is made by God and is perfect for our elevation. Therefore, the change we need to bring about in our lives must begin from within.

AFFLICTIONS OF THE MIND

In the last chapter, we learned how our thoughts can make us either happy or sad. These thoughts pour forth in a constant stream. Let us say that it's the weekend and we glance outside. We see that a nice summer day is ahead of us. We happily recall our plans to take a pleasant hike in the woods with some friends. Then a thought about layoffs in the next few months at work pops into our mind, and we sink into a gloomy mood. Thoughts of doubt and fear rush through our mind and occupy us for several minutes.

Finally, we put the matter out of our mind, and another thought pops up unexpectedly. We forgot to go to the store yesterday to pick up bread for breakfast. Do we have time? Yes, just enough. So we dash out of the door to go to the store. On the way, multitudes of thoughts run through our mind: the road has a pothole; the driver in front is too slow; is there anything else to get from the store? And so it goes on and on, incessantly, day after day, thought after thought after thought.

One guru called his disciples around him. He related a hilarious joke that made them all laugh. The guru then proceeded to relate the same anecdote again. This time, some sniggered while others smiled politely. But the guru did not stop there; he went on to repeat the same joke before them. This time, they could only manage a sheepish grin.

Not to be discouraged, he related the anecdote once again. Now, one of the students could not restrain herself anymore. She said, 'Gurudev, your joke has become very boring. You have already repeated it four times.'

The guru replied, 'If you get bored listening to a hilarious joke again and again, then why do you go on recalling thoughts of fear, misery, and hurt in your mind?'

Is there any way to control the constant flow of thoughts within us? The subtle machine inside that generates thoughts is the mind, and hence, the key to controlling and managing thoughts will come with a deeper understanding of the functioning of the mind.

Theories About the Mind

How does the mind function, and what is its correlation to the behavioural traits of people? Psychology is a branch of human knowledge that attempts to analyse the science of the mind and behaviour by establishing general principles and researching specific cases. It is recognised as an academic discipline as well as an applied science. Allied to it are branches of psychoanalysis, psychotherapy, psychodynamics, psychiatry, and many more.

Some of the more popular branches of psychology are shared here.

Psychoanalysis

It was Sigmund Freud who first made Western psychology famous. Freud, better known as 'Father of Psychoanalysis', was the first to introduce the concept of an unconscious mind. At the end of the nineteenth century, he presented his theory of psychoanalysis in Austria.

Psychoanalysis is the study of the theories and therapeutic techniques that aim to explore and cure the unconscious mind. According to Freudian psychoanalysis, the human psyche comprises of id, ego, and superego. The 'id' refers to the inherent drives we seek to fulfil because we believe that by doing so, we will be happier. The 'superego' is our value system. It is partially learned in childhood, and is partially an inherent value system. The 'ego' is the mediator between the superego and id and works on the 'reality principle' i.e. it helps us determine which drives to act upon. Freud theorised that conflict between them results in disorders.

Analytical Psychology

This is the school of psychology founded by Carl Jung. Early in his career, Jung was a close associate of Freud. The two had a great rapport and, at one point, Freud considered Jung as his successor. However, Jung's ideas later began to diverge from Freud's, and the two broke away.

There were two key points of contention between them: a) Freud focused on the unconscious as a repository of negative emotions, while Jung considered the unconscious as 'collective' and 'personal' because he believed it contained memory and ideas inherited from ancestors; and b) Freud's theory focused on sexual development while Jung focused on the 'collective unconscious' or universal symbols that all can relate to.

The primary goal of life, according to Jungian psychology, is the individuation of the self with both its conscious and unconscious aspects. The unconscious can be related to or understood via symbols seen in daily life, such as in dreams, art, religion, personal relationships, and so on. The process of bridging the conscious and the unconscious together leads to harmony; obstacles or disruptions can result in disorders.

Cognitive Psychology

It is the field of psychology that aims to understand our higher-level mental processes, such as attention, creativity, language, memory, perception, problem-solving, thinking, and their impact on behaviour. Among other things, these processes involve the use of sensory memory, short-term memory, and long-term memory.

The process of language acquisition, the impact of language on mood and behaviour, and other related topics are helping researchers identify learning disabilities at an early age. The studies on attention and memory have led to significant gains in treating Attention Deficit Hyperactivity Disorder (ADHD). With such relevant topics and backed by scientific research, cognitive psychology quickly gained credibility and application. Other branches of psychology such as abnormal psychology, developmental psychology, and social psychology, and the fields of economics and linguistics draw heavily from cognitive psychology.

Behaviourism

This branch of psychology disagrees with the psychoanalytical approach of introspection and focuses on how external environments impact behaviour. B.F. Skinner's 'operant conditioning' model accepted and acknowledged the role of thoughts and emotions as influencing one's behaviour. This was in contrast to the previous theory of 'classical conditioning' that focused only on external stimuli.

Behaviourism, together with cognitive psychology, is widely used as Cognitive Behaviour Therapy (CBT) to treat disorders, such as anxiety, depression, mood disorders, phobias, and Post-Traumatic Stress Disorder (PTSD), among others.

Humanistic Psychology

While Carl Rogers is widely credited with the establishment of humanistic psychology, it was Abraham Maslow's 'Hierarchy of Needs' that brought it to the forefront as a distinct branch. Psychologists affiliated with this branch emphasise human beings as more than the sum of their parts. As a result, instead of focusing on one mental affliction, they prefer to view the individual as a whole.

According to Maslow, we all have basic physiological needs, such as hunger, thirst, sex, and sleep, among other necessities. As these are fulfilled, safety and security needs of job security, safety of home, and so on, start becoming important. As these needs are satisfied, the need for love and belonging starts gaining prominence. Beyond this is the need for achievement and respect. And lastly, is the need for self-actualisation where one is working purely for the joy of it.

Existential Psychology

This branch of psychology is most concerned with fulfilling one's meaning in life. Essentially, it looks for universal principles that apply to all instead of isolating people or their behavioural patterns. Existential psychology lists the four dimensions of human life: physical (relationship to one's physical self, health and wellbeing, relationship with the external environment), social (relationship with others), psychological (focus on one's attitude and experiences), and spiritual (relationship with the unknown or discovering the meaning of one's life in a more personal way).

Viktor Frankl is one of the most famous existential psychologists, who later broke away and developed a branch of therapy called 'logotherapy'.

Positive Psychology

As recently as 1998, Martin Seligman formalised positive psychology as a valid branch of psychology. Together with Mihaly Csikszentmihalyi, he defined positive psychology as 'the scientific study of positive human functioning and flourishing on multiple levels that include the biological, personal, relational, institutional, cultural, and global dimensions of life.'

The basic premise here is to look to the future to live a happy and meaningful life. By doing so, one learns to focus on the positive. This is in stark contrast to other branches of psychology that focus on disorders of the mind.

As you can see from the above, there is a plethora of perspectives on the functioning of the mind. These are helpful branches of psychology. However, truly meaningful and lasting improvements to the mind's activity cannot be accomplished without a profound comprehension of the mind in the context of all creation.

In this book, we will learn the science of the mind and intellect as contained in the ancient Vedic texts. In this divine light, we will discover practical tools to use in everyday circumstances and situations. These tools will help us to not only lead a better life, but also to fulfil the objective of our sojourn on Planet Earth.

The Ancient Science of Vedic Psychology

Astonishingly, the science of the mind was perfectly explained 5,000 years ago in the ancient Vedic scriptures. This science, which we can call Vedic psychology, describes the mind's working so clearly that, in contrast, the empirical theories of modern psychology pale into insignificance.

Vedic psychology is elaborated in great detail in the Upanishads and the Bhagavad Gita, along with other Vedic scriptures. These ancient texts have been greatly acclaimed by several famous western scholars. To quote a few:

> Whenever I have read any part of the Vedas, I have felt that a divine light illuminated me. In the great teaching of the Vedas, there is no touch of sectarianism.
>
> *Henry David Thoreau, American writer and philosopher*

> When we read the philosophical monuments of the East, above all, those of India, we discover in them, many truths so highly elevated in contrast to which the European genius

has stopped, that we are constrained to bend our knees before the philosophy of India.

Victor Cousin, French philosopher

When I read the Bhagavad Gita, and reflect about how God created this universe, everything else seems so superfluous.

Albert Einstein, American scientist

There is nothing in this world as elevating as the Upaniṣhads. They have been the solace of my life and they shall be the solace of my death.

Arthur Schopenhauer, German philosopher

If these words of Schopenhauer require any confirmation, I shall gladly give it as the result of my lifelong study of the Vedic scriptures.

Professor Max Müller, German Orientalist

Eternal philosophical truth has seldom found a more striking and decisive expression than in the emancipating knowledge of the philosophy of the Upaniṣhads.

Paul Deussen, German Orientalist

Access to the Vedas is the greatest privilege this century may claim over previous centuries.

J Robert Oppenheimer, American nuclear physicist

The Bhagavad Gita is one of the clearest and most comprehensive summaries of the perennial philosophy ever to have been done.

Aldous Huxley, English writer

Vedic psychology presents the origin and creation of mental afflictions in a systematic, scientific, and logical manner.

It further teaches us the techniques for purification of the mind and the solution to problems of everyday life through improvement in our thinking.

Let us embark on a thrilling journey on the pathways of Vedic psychology. I assure you that it could be the most rewarding journey of your life. But the subtle science requires an open mind, concentration, and dedication to understand it. Therefore, patiently read the logic enumerated here, down to the last link, and you will find that all the pieces of the jigsaw puzzle of the mind's functioning fall neatly into place.

Diseases of the Mind

We are familiar with bodily afflictions and their consequences. A single physical ailment has the capacity to ruin our entire day. It is not uncommon to hear people say that their back was aching or head was dizzy, and so they could do nothing throughout the day. However, physical ailments are not even fractionally as debilitating as mental ones. Sage Tulsidas states:

eka vyādhi vaśha nara marahiñ, ye asādhi bahu vyādhi
pīṛahin santata jīva kahuñ, so kimi lahai samādhi

(Ramayan)

'Even one physical ailment is enough to incapacitate us. Then think of the plight of the soul afflicted by numerous mental ailments. Is there a means for relief?'

The Vedic scriptures refer to anger, envy, greed, desire, among other weaknesses as *mānas rog* (mental illnesses). They afflict all of us as long as we are in the world of maya.

The problem is that we often do not even realise that we have a mental affliction. We know we get angry, and we are aware that we become envious as well, but we do not know that anger and envy are diseased conditions. Instead, we write them off as 'human nature' or a 'natural tendency'. And since we are unaware of their effect on our overall health and wellbeing, we do not try to cure them.

These mental diseases are so overpowering that even government laws are unable to keep them in check. People know that violence can result in imprisonment, and yet when angry, they do not hesitate to transgress the law. They know that the consumption of narcotics is illegal, but still, driven by desire, they remain addicted. Why? Why is it that we behave in ways that do us more harm than good?

To answer this question, let us study the diseases of the mind—one at a time.

The Disease of Anger

One of the grossest mental afflictions is anger. When it arises, it disturbs our inner poise. It causes a rush of blood to the head. We often regret what we say or do when we are in a rage. Later, we wish that we had not become angry, and we wonder how we succumbed to it. The backlash of anger can remain inside us for much longer than the provocation that caused it.

Rosh was changing the punctured tyre of his car that was parked outside his home. Unknown to him, his son had taken a sharp-edged stone and was etching graffiti on the other side of the car. After replacing the wheel, Rosh walked around and discovered the damage that his five-year-old son had done. Rosh became livid with rage. He took the spanner in his hand and began beating his son mercilessly on his knuckles. Though the son screamed, Rosh continued slamming his hand in his fit of fury.

Later, Rosh discovered that he had broken the fingers of his little boy. He rushed him to the hospital. The doctor examined the hand and said that a couple of fingers would have to be removed to avoid gangrene from growing on the dead mass. Rosh was shattered at what he had done.

After the surgery, when the little boy regained consciousness, he looked at his hand and asked innocently, 'Father, when will my fingers grow back?' Rosh broke down in tears. He returned home, filled with remorse.

In the driveway, his eyes fell on the graffiti on the car. His son had written, 'I love you, Dad.' The child had innocently expressed his love by scratching the car. But in his rage, Rosh had behaved like a fiend.

Such is the nature of anger. It makes us forget civility, good manners, and kindness. In its grip, humans forget basic respect, empathy, and compassion. Hence, the Sanskrit saying: *krodhāt krodhe kathannute.* 'Do not allow anger to overcome you, rather, become angry upon anger itself.'

The question now before us is this: How can we overcome anger? Nobody wants to become a slave of fury and allow the intellect to be deluded by it. Yet, when it attacks us, we forget and make the mistake of giving into it. Why does anger arise and is there any permanent solution to overcome it?

In order to answer this question, we first need to understand another mental affliction.

The Disease of Greed

A second mental disease is greed—for money, prestige, delicacies, luxurious objects, or anything else. Though people spend their whole life striving to satiate greed, it remains forever unfulfilled like a bottomless vessel. Unlike anger that reaches a peak and then subsides, greed never diminishes, and motivated by it, we burn out, as is seen in the rat-race of the corporate world.

Let me share a powerful story on this topic.

A king was hunting alone in a dense forest when he lost his way. Wandering desperately, he reached the hut of a villager called Lobhiram, who gave him food, drink, and shelter for the night. The next morning, the king thanked him from the bottom of his heart and offered him the boon of his choice.

Lobhiram said, 'O King, yours is a large kingdom. Please grant me the boon that all the land I can measure with my horse from sunrise to sunset should be mine.'

The king, out of gratitude to the villager, consented, 'So be it.'

The next day, Lobhiram started off from outside the king's capital city. He had a good steed and he kept prodding it to gallop as fast as it could. By ten o'clock in the morning, he had covered a huge terrain. The land would have sufficed for him and many generations of his progeny, but it was insufficient for his greed. By midday, both the rider and the horse were exhausted, and their throats were parched like leather, but Lobhiram's greed was ever fresh and yearning for more. Finally, in the late afternoon, the steed collapsed. Lobhiram was thrown off and crashed headlong into a boulder by the side of the road. He died on the spot.

When nearby villagers came to bury Lobhiram, they exclaimed, 'Alas! In the end, just these two yards of land alone were useful to him. All the rest was wasted.'

Such is the nature of greed—it drives us unforgivingly for fulfilment of desires—which never happens.

The *Garuḍ Purāṇ* states:

chakradharo 'pi suratvaṁ suratvalābhe sakalasurapatitvam
surapatirūrdhvagatitvaṁ tathāpi nanivartate tṛiṣhṇā
(2.12.14)

'A king wishes to be the emperor of the world; the emperor aspires to be a celestial god; a celestial god seeks to be Indra, the king of heaven; and Indra desires to be Brahma, the secondary creator. Yet, the thirst for material enjoyment does not get satiated.'

The difference between our needs and our wants is created by greed. We do not need much to live a happy life. But greed creates innumerable wants for more wealth, higher posts, greater prestige, and bigger houses. The more we get, the more we want; nothing seems to quell our discontentment. Imagine just how blissful life would be with the wealth of inner contentment that would come if we could free ourselves from greed.

What is the origin of greed and what is its cure? The answer to this question will become abundantly clear in just a little while. Read on patiently.

The Affliction of Desire

Both anger and greed are severe afflictions of the mind. Yet, the Vedas say that these are both marginal; more perilous than even these is another disease. What is that? Desire!

To want, long, or hope for something is *kāmanā* (desire). It is fundamentally of five kinds: the desire to see, the desire to hear, the desire to smell, the desire to taste, and the desire to touch. Together, these are called *kām* (lust), and referred to by one word, 'desire'.

How dangerous is desire? The *Sūkti Sudhākar* states:

kuraṅga mātaṅga pataṅga bhṛiṅga,
mīnāhatāḥ pañchabhireva pañcha
ekaḥ pramādī sa kathaṁ na hanyate,
yaḥ sevate pañchabhireva pañcha

This popular verse translates as follows:

- 'The deer loves music for the pleasure of the ear. It is enticed by the hunter, who plays melodious music, and shoots the deer when it comes to hear it.
- 'The elephant loves the tactile enjoyment it gets from its skin. It is allured into the net by the female elephant and becomes easy prey for the waiting poacher.
- 'The moth lusts for the light to gratify its eyes. It is drawn to the flame and gets burned alive.

- 'The bee loves fragrance, for it gives pleasure to its nostrils. It refuses to fly off when the flower closes at sunset and gets trapped within.
- 'The fish, yearning for indulgence of its tongue, nibbles at the bait and ends up in the fisherman's frying pan.

All these die in pursuit of the pleasure of one of the senses. What will happen to the human who is chasing all five objects of gratification?'

Desire is universally singled out in all the Vedic scriptures as the worst mental affliction. We may wonder why it is considered such a big culprit. In anger, people destroy life and property. In greed, they waste their whole life accumulating meaningless goods and posts they could easily live without. But in desire, they only hanker for gratification and indulgence. So, isn't desire relatively innocuous in comparison to anger and greed?

No, it is not, for desire is the mother of anger and greed. Let us understand this in the following sections.

Anger Arises from Desire

Let us understand the origin of anger through the following story:

Chandu developed a deep desire to eat ice cream. He purchased two litres of Chocolate Chip from the local ice cream store and placed it in the freezer. Chandu then went for a walk in the sun to work up an appetite, so that he could really enjoy the ice cream on his return. However, on coming back, he found that there was no ice cream in the refrigerator.

'I had put a large pack of ice cream here,' Chandu exclaimed. 'Where did it go?'

'My dear husband, do you not remember?' his wife commented nonchalantly. 'The doctor had prescribed that you should limit your sugar intake. I have trashed the ice cream.'

'What? You threw the ice cream?' Chandu yelled. He became incensed with rage upon his wife.

What was the cause for Chandu's outburst? He had created a desire and its fulfilment was obstructed by his wife. This led to the anger outburst. Therefore, anger comes not on its own, but from the obstruction of desire.

Consider other examples:

- We grow angry when we want our family to concur with our views and they do not.
- We become angry when others refuse to follow our suggestions or instructions.

Thus, desire is the mother and anger is its child. Sometimes people come to me, saying, 'Swami-ji, everything is okay in me except for anger.'

'You do not have any affliction apart from anger?' I ask.

'No, Swami-ji. Anger is my only problem.'

'Impossible! If anger is present, its cause, desire, must also be present.'

We have learned that **the cause for anger is the obstruction of desire.** Now let us determine the cause for greed.

Greed Also Arises from Desire

Let us go back to the example of Chandu and his wife. We had seen how, when Chandu discovered his wife had trashed the ice cream he craved, he had become livid with rage.

Now, suppose, the wife did not throw the ice cream. When Chandu returned, he began eating voraciously.

Now, ask him, 'Did you enjoy the ice cream?'

'Yes.'

'So, is your desire satiated forever?'

'No, it is only satiated for today,' he replies. 'After three days, I will want it again.'

This example illustrates how fulfilling desire only extinguishes it for a brief moment. It then comes back with greater intensity. In this way, the fulfilment of desire is the cause of greed.

The uncommonly known secret of this world is that desire can never be eliminated by satiating it. It is like attempting to extinguish a fire by pouring clarified butter on it. The fire does seem to go away, but only momentarily. It then flares up with redoubled vigour.

Thus, like anger, greed is also the child of desire. The Ramayan states:

jimi pratilābha lobha adhikāī

'If you satisfy desire, it results in greed.'

The Shreemad Bhagavatam states:

yat pṛithivyāṁ vrīhi-yavaṁ hiraṇyaṁ paśhavaḥ striyaḥ
na duhyanti manaḥ-prītiṁ puṁsaḥ kāma-hatasya te
(9.19.13)

'If one person was to get all the wealth, luxuries, and sensual objects in the world, that person's desire would still not be satiated. Hence, knowing it to be the cause of misery, an intelligent person should renounce desire.'

The Puranas relate a powerful story about how desires get inflamed.

Saubhari was a great sage in ancient times. He is mentioned in the Ṛig Veda, *where there is a mantra called* Saubhari Sūtra. *There is also a scripture called the* Saubhari Samhitā. *In other words, he was not just another hermit. Saubhari had attained such control over his body that he could submerge himself in the Yamuna and meditate under water. One day, he saw two fish mating. This spectacle carried away his mind and senses, and the desire for sexual consummation arose in him. He abandoned his spiritual practice and came out of the water, wondering how to fulfil his desire.*

At that time, the king of Ayodhya was Maandhata, a very illustrious and noble ruler. He had fifty daughters, each more beautiful than the other. Saubhari approached the king and asked for the hand in marriage of one of the fifty princesses.

King Maandhata wondered about the sanity of the sage and thought to himself, 'An old man wanting to get married!' The king knew Saubhari to be a powerful sage, and feared that if he refused, the sage might curse him. But if he consented, the life of one of his daughters would be ruined. He was in a dilemma. As a way out of the predicament, he said, 'O holy one! I have no objection to your request. Please take a seat. I shall bring my fifty daughters before you, and whosoever chooses you will become yours in marriage.' The king was confident that none of his daughters would choose the old ascetic, and in this way, he would be saved from the sage's curse.

Saubhari was all too aware of the king's intention. He told the king that he would return the following day. That evening, he used his yogic powers to turn himself into a handsome young man. Consequently, when he presented himself at the palace the next day, all the fifty princesses chose him as their husband. The king was bound by the word he had given and was compelled to marry all his daughters to the sage.

Now the king was deeply concerned about how Sage Saubhari could keep his fifty daughters happy. However, Saubhari again used his yogic powers. Putting the king's apprehension to rest, he assumed fifty forms, created fifty palaces for his wives, and lived separately with each of them. In this manner, thousands of years passed by. The Puranas state that Saubhari had many children from each of them, and those children had further children, until a tiny city was created!

One day, Saubhari came to his senses, and exclaimed: aho imaṁ paśhyata me vināśhaṁ (Shreemad Bhagavatam 9.6.50) *'O humans! Those of you, who make plans to attain happiness through material acquisitions, be careful. Look at my degradation—I used to sit in samadhi in the Yamuna. One desire arose, and to satiate it, I created fifty bodies by my yogic powers, living with fifty women for thousands of years. And yet, the senses did not experience fulfilment; they only kept hankering for more. Learn from my downfall and be not fooled into thinking you will ever fulfil desire.'*

Saubhari realised he had been chasing a mirage.

Worldly pleasures have also been called *mṛiga tṛiṣhṇā* in the scriptures which means 'like a mirage seen by the deer'. The sun's rays reflecting on the hot desert sand create an illusion of water. The deer, fooled by the illusion, thinks there is water ahead of it and runs to quench its thirst. Its dull intellect cannot realise it is the victim of deception. The more it runs towards the water, the further the mirage recedes. The unfortunate deer keeps chasing the illusory water and finally dies of exhaustion.

Likewise, material energy, maya, too creates an illusion of happiness. And we run after that illusory happiness in the hope of quenching the thirst of our senses. But no matter how much we try, happiness recedes from us.

We see how the wealthy have enough food and clothes for survival, and yet they remain disturbed and unsatisfied. They see someone else with a better house, better clothes, a more lucrative job, and so there is no contentment.

These desires can also be compared to an itch. When we have an itch, it creates an irresistible urge to scratch. But scratching does not solve the problem. There is relief for a while, and then the desire to scratch returns with greater force. Instead, if one tolerates the itch for some time, the urge to scratch dies down slowly.

5

The same logic applies to desires as well. The mind and senses throw up myriad wishes for happiness. As long as we are in the game of fulfilling them, they flare endlessly. However, when we learn to turn the mind away from material allurements and renounce the desires of the senses, we come in touch with the inner bliss of the soul.

The *Kaṭhopaniṣhad* goes to the extent of saying that one who has renounced sensual desires becomes like God:

yadā sarve pramuchyante kāmā ye 'sya hṛidi śhritaḥ
atha martyo 'mṛito bhavatyatra brahma samaśhnute
(2.3.14)

'When one eliminates all selfish desires from the heart, then the materially fettered *jīvātmā* (soul) attains freedom from birth and death and becomes godlike in virtue.' The godlike nature of the soul that is devoid of yearning is also stated in the Shreemad Bhagavatam:

vimuñchati yadā kāmān mānavo manasi sthitān
tarhyeva puṇḍarīkākṣha bhagavattvāya kalpate (7.10.9)

'That person who eradicates wants and becomes situated in a state of contentment becomes like God.'

The Bhagavad Gita also states:

vihāya kāmān yaḥ sarvān pumānśh charati niḥspṛihaḥ
nirmamo nirahankāraḥ sa śhāntim adhigachchhati (2.71)

'One who gives up all material desires and lives free from a sense of greed, proprietorship, and egoism, attains perfect peace.'

Elimination of desire is also the focus of the Buddhist philosophy. The four noble truths, so strongly emphasised by the Buddha, are:

1) There is misery in the world
2) Misery has a cause.
3) The cause of misery is desire.
4) If desire is eradicated, misery will be eradicated.

The downward spiral beginning from desire does not end merely with anger and greed. Let us see how far downhill it can take us.

Anger Destroys Good Judgement

We have seen how desire is like a two-edged sword. Its fulfilment leads to greed and its hindrance leads to anger. Once anger arises, it brings with it numerous other afflictions. Lord Krishna states:

krodhād bhavati sammohaḥ sammohāt smṛiti-vibhramaḥ
smṛiti-bhranśhād buddhi-nāśho buddhi-nāśhāt praṇaśhyati

(Bhagavad Gita 2.63)

'Anger leads to veiling of judgement, which results in bewilderment of memory. When the memory is bewildered, the intellect gets destroyed; and when the intellect is destroyed, one is ruined.'

Anger clouds the intellect, just as the morning mist creates a hazy covering on sunlight. When the intellect is shrouded, it leads to bewilderment of memory. The person then forgets what is right and what is wrong and flows along with the surge of emotions. Bewilderment of memory results in destruction of the intellect. Since intellect is our internal guide, when it gets destroyed, one is ruined.

In this manner, a host of mental afflictions arise from desire. Now, let us look at the reverse of this. If we eradicate desire, greed will naturally disappear and so will anger. In that case, none of the other sequential afflictions after anger will arise. The mind will be mastered merely by the conquest of desire.

If desire is the cause of all problems, let us see what is it that gives rise to desire.

The Malady of Attachment

We all experience different desires. While reading this book, someone's mind may wander to tea, another's mind may start thinking of cricket, while yet another's mind may ramble towards her child. Why is it that the mind of individuals generates such dissimilar desires?

What is causing this variety of cravings? One person desires prestige to the extent that he is willing to give fifteen lectures a day to get elected. Another desires money to the extent that he neglects his family to earn it. The third desires his paramour and is willing to sacrifice all his wealth on her. Where does desire originate from?

The answer is that when our mind is attached to something, we experience desire for it. The cause of desire is attachment. The mind is a frequent visitor to the things and people it is most devoted to. In other words, if one is attached to alcohol, the desire for alcohol comes frequently to the mind. If attached to cigarettes, then thoughts of the pleasure of smoking cigarettes continually flow in the mind, creating a craving for them. In this way, attachment leads to desire.

This point may seem to go against common sense. It would seem logical to think that the intrinsic qualities of an object make us desire it. But this is really not the case.

For example, alcohol has no attractive aroma. It is foul smelling and obnoxious, and the very first time we taste it, we actually do not like it. Yet, the same foul smell is so enticing to an alcoholic that, when he passes by the pub, he begins swaying. The odour of alcohol, which makes one want to vomit, sparks the other's craving. The difference is due to attachment. The alcoholic's craving is coming from his attachment to alcohol.

Here is another example.

Is the smoke from cigarettes pleasant or filthy? You may say, 'It is awful. It makes me want to turn around and go the other way.' Then, why is it so attractive to the addict? Because of his own attachment to it. It is not the intrinsic property of cigarettes, but the attachment within the addict's mind that creates a craving for them.

Let me repeat this for emphasis. **It is our attachment to an object, not its intrinsic properties, which create desire for it.** Let me cite yet another example.

A mother lost her child in a fair. She went to the police booth and filed a complaint about her missing child. The policeman said, 'Mother, four lost-and-found children have been brought to our booth. See which of these kids is yours.'

The mother looked at all of them and responded, 'None of these is my child.'

'But you saw such beautiful children,' said the policeman. 'Why don't you pick any of them and hug her with maternal affection? Why are you hankering for your child alone?'

The mother replied, 'Mr Policeman, you will never understand the heart of a mother. I will only be able to sleep after I see my little child.'

The mother does not want beauty. She wants **her** child to whom her mind is attached.

Thus, the cause of desire is determined—it is attachment. The full link is now clear. If we harbour attachment, it will lead to desire; from desire will arise anger and greed. From anger will arise subsequent afflictions like illusion. Conversely, if we can eliminate attachment, there will be no scope for desire, and all subsequent afflictions will automatically cease.

This brings us to the million-dollar question: What is the cause of attachment? The next section explains it.

The Impact of Repetitive Thinking

Not everyone's mind is attached to the same thing. Someone is so committed to golf that his wife is practically a golf-widow. The other is so attached to his wife that he spends all his money on pleasing her. The third is so devoted to money that he has no time to spend with his family. We all have different attachments. Let us try to understand their source.

When our mind repeatedly revises the thought, 'there is happiness in this object or person', our mind develops attachment to that object or person.

For example, in a class many boys and girls interact innocuously with each other. One day, one boy notices something about a girl and starts thinking, 'I would be very happy if she were mine.' As he continuously repeats this thought, his mind becomes attached to her. He tells his friends that he is madly in love with her, and he is unable to study because his mind repeatedly thinks about her. His friends ridicule him that they all interact with her in class, but none of them is crazy about her. Why is he losing his sleep and ruining his grades thinking of her? The reason is that he repeatedly contemplated happiness in the girl, and as a result, his mind became attached to her.

Consider a second example illustrating how attachment develops.

How does one become attached to alcohol? There is no one who says in the beginning itself, 'Get me the bottle! I cannot live without it.' Rather, on the first day, alcohol tastes awful and people force themselves to drink it. Nevertheless, their friends convince them, 'We all get great pleasure from whisky. Drink and enjoy life!'

Ill-advised by others, a person thinks, 'My friends are loving it. I will too.' He tries a drink and gets a tiny kick from the inebriation of the brain. The person begins contemplating happiness in the feeling of mental lightness. The more he consumes alcohol, the more he contemplates happiness in it, and the deeper the attachment grows, until finally, he becomes an alcoholic.

Then the same person who had forced himself to drink on the first day now says, 'I do not care about my family. Let my business get ruined. Never mind if my liver is spoiled! But give me the fifth peg of vodka ... I cannot live without it!' How did this transformation take place? It was his own repeated thinking of happiness in alcohol that led to the addiction.

Now the full link is clear. This chain of causation is also stated in the Bhagavad Gita:

dhyāyato viṣhayān puṁsaḥ saṅgas teṣhūpajāyate
saṅgāt sañjāyate kāmaḥ kāmāt krodho 'bhijāyate (2.62)

'By repeated contemplation of happiness in the objects of the senses, one develops attachment to them. Attachment creates desire, and from desire arises anger.'

Why We All Seek Happiness

We have seen how the chain of mental afflictions begins with the contemplation of happiness. Let us now come to the last link in this chain. Why do we seek happiness? We try to find it in our family, work, hobbies, activities, and in everything else we do. Yet it eludes us. Even after so many disappointments, why do we not stop seeking happiness?

The Vedas state: *ānando brahmeti vyajānāt*. 'Know God to be of the nature of Bliss.' The Supreme Lord is an infinite ocean of divine bliss, and we souls are His fragmental parts. By nature, each part is spontaneously attracted towards its source. A lump of mud is a part of the earth and is pulled towards it by the force of gravity. A river is created by water vapour arising from the sea, and it flows back into the sea. Similarly, we souls are little drops of the ocean of infinite happiness, and hence, our natural propensity is to seek bliss. Until we get the infinite happiness of God, we will not be content.

In other words, until the part, our tiny soul, attains the whole, the Supreme Soul, we will not stop our quest for happiness. Somewhere or the other we will contemplate bliss, and once that happens, the whole chain of attachment, desire, anger, and greed will naturally follow.

We have understood that to seek bliss is our inherent nature; we cannot change it. How, then, can we rise above these mental afflictions? The solution to this problem is actually very simple.

Replace Lower Attachments with Higher Ones

The urge for happiness is as natural to the soul as thirst is to the physical body. It is impossible to think, 'I will not contemplate happiness anywhere.' The simple solution then is to envision happiness in beneficial things. Cultivate virtuous desires, such as the desire for inner growth, austerity, service, and sacrifice.

For example, if we repeatedly think that happiness is in becoming wise, we will become attached to good knowledge. This will lead to the yearning to gather more knowledge. The desire for knowledge—which is good—will not bind us; rather, it will uplift us.

Similarly, if we contemplate happiness in good health, we will become devoted to it. This will make us crave wellness for ourselves. Such desire will only help us become healthier.

The same principle can be used to develop love for the Supreme. If we repeatedly think that happiness is in the Supreme Divine Lord, we will become attached to Him. The mind will then hanker for the Supreme Lord. The Shreemad Bhagavatam states:

viṣhayān dhyāyataśh chittaṁ viṣhayeṣhu viṣhajjate
mām anusmarataśh chittaṁ mayy eva pravilīyate

(11.14.27)

'You repeatedly thought of the pleasures in the objects of the senses and became attached to them. Now frequently think that God is the ocean of infinite bliss, and you will develop devotion towards Him.'

The process is the same; we only need to change the direction. Saint Ramakrishna Paramahamsa expressed this principle very eloquently when he said:

> Devotion is love for the highest; and the lowest shall fall away by itself.

The great saints in history were not free from desire, instead, their desire was millions of times stronger than ours. The only difference was that while we desired the world, they desired to love the Lord with all their heart and serve Him with their every act.

Attachment to the Supreme does not spoil the mind like material attachment, rather, it purifies the mind. God is all-pure, and when we attach our mind to Him, it gets cleansed. The Bhagavad Gita states:

> *mām̐ cha yo 'vyabhichāreṇa bhakti-yogena sevate*
> *sa guṇān samatītyaitān brahma-bhūyāya kalpate* (14.26)

'Those who attach their minds to Me with unadulterated devotion rise above the three modes of material nature and attain the level of the Supreme Brahman.'

While material desires bind the soul, noble desires uplift us. Where does that leave anger and greed?

Make Anger Your Friend

We have seen that desire leads to anger and greed. The desire for noble things is no exception to this rule. When it is not fulfilled, the devotee also feels anger. The key is to channel this anger in the proper direction. Thus, in the Ramayan, a devotee of Lord Ram says:

ha raghunandana prāna pirīte,
tumha binu jiata bahuta dina bīte

'O Lord Ram, how heartless I am that, without your devotion, I still continue to live.' When anger is directed constructively, it propels us more rapidly on the upward path. If we become angry at ourselves for the lack of improvement, we strive to try harder. We refuse to compromise and prod our mind forward and upward. In this way, by channelling anger in the proper manner, we can make it our friend.

Make Greed Your Friend

We have learned that the fulfilment of desire leads to greed. Similarly, sublime desires lead to divine greed. The devotee yearns for more devotion, more divine knowledge, and more service. Such greed is very helpful since it keeps one hungry for further progress. In this fashion, a devotee says:

sītā rāma charana rati moreñ,
anudina baṛhaụ anugraha toreñ (Ramayan)

'O Sita Ram, I pray that my loving devotion at Your feet may increase day and night.' This is sublime greed, which is no longer detrimental; instead, it elevates one to even greater spiritual heights.

What about envy? Like the rest, if it is properly oriented, it becomes helpful. When we see others ahead of us in spiritual growth, we should think, 'She began attending JKYog's Life Transformation Programmes (LTP) along with me. She has progressed so rapidly and developed such immense patience and tolerance. Why am I left behind? I too must try harder for self-improvement.'

Make Pride Your Frienu

The biggest of all material defects is pride which is extremely difficult to overcome. People become scholars of the scriptures and masters of austerity, and yet remain full of pride. Once again, the ego can be neutralised easily by dovetailing it towards the Supreme. Expressing this sentiment, Hanuman says:

asa abhimāna jāi jani bhorey,
maiñ sevaka raghupati pati morey (Ramayan)

'May this pride never leave me that my Master is the great Lord Ram, and I am the servant of such a great Master.' **Pride in the Lord strengthens faith and enthusiasm for devotion.**

We have seen how all the mental afflictions—the worst enemies within—become our best friends when they are properly directed. This is powerful information for changing ourselves!

Now, for internal transformation to be permanent and not fleeting, we must tap into the power of habits. How do we dismantle old habits and develop beneficial ones? Let us discuss how we can install great habits within ourselves.

SUMMARY OF THE MAIN POINTS

» Like physical diseases, there are also afflictions of the mind. Anger, greed, desire, envy, and pride, among other human failings, are all mental afflictions. They are far more impactful than bodily ailments.

» Anger does not come by itself. It is caused when we harbour a desire and its fulfilment is obstructed.

» Desire is such a disease that it can never be satiated . The more we fulfil it, the more it gets inflamed. Hence greed comes from the station of desire.

» Desire arises out of attachment to objects or people.

» Attachment happens when we repeatedly contemplate happiness somewhere.

» It is impossible for the soul not to contemplate happiness. The ocean of happiness is God Himself, and since the soul is a part of God, it naturally seeks happiness. The solution then is to seek happiness in the proper direction.

» Repeated contemplation of happiness in God will lead to attachment to Him. This will result in dovetailing desires in the direction of God.

» Since God is all-pure, desire for Him does not degrade the mind. Rather, it becomes purified in devotion to Him

THE POWER OF HABITS

What is a habit? Simply put, it is a person's customary way of thinking or behaving. Habitual behaviour is natural or automatic and does not demand self-analysis. For better or for worse, habits become a part of who we are and constitute an intrinsic aspect of our personality.

For example, those who are habituated to drinking bed-tea find it difficult to get out of bed without their morning cup, Those who are accustomed to a game of tennis after office feel uneasy on rainy days when they cannot play. Those who have the habit of drinking wine with their meal cannot swallow their dinner without it. And those who are used to uplifting their mind through daily sadhana, or spiritual practice. feel uncomfortable if they miss it even a single day.

The Power of Conditioning

In India's Gajapati district of Southern Odisha, is an area at the base of Mahendragiri Hills, where elephants are trained. I once visited Mahendragiri and found a row of elephants roped to wooden stakes dug into the earth. I asked the mahout (elephant caretaker) about the secret of the elephants' docility.

The mahout explained, 'Swami-ji, when the elephant is a baby, it is tied with ropes to a stake. Initially, it is not used to being secured, so it pulls and pulls. Since it is weak and the rope is strong, it keeps tugging in vain till a day comes when it realises that no tugging will help. Then, it stops and stands still. Now it is "conditioned". Later, when it becomes a huge and mighty adult tusker, it is still tied with the rope to the stake. With one tug, it could walk away to freedom, but it goes nowhere because it has been "conditioned".'

We humans too tend to behave according to our habitual conditioning. We act through the force of habit as our mind is conditioned. As humans we are free to choose differently, but rarely do we consider the available alternatives.

Our everyday attitudes also come from mental conditioning. If we have habituated our mind to see the positive side of things, we are likely to remain cheerful and optimistic even when difficult situations arise. If we have accustomed our mind to doubt or to see the worst in others, we will habitually suspect even their best-intentioned actions. Similarly, thoughts of generosity, empathy, fear, and envy also come to us from habitual thought patterns. **First, we mould our habits, and later, our habits mould us.**

Why do habits grip us so powerfully? This is because of the way in which the brain has been hardwired. Let us understand how.

The Neuroplastic Nature of the Brain

The science of neurology says the human brain is endowed with a hundred billion neurons. These combine with each other to form trillions of neural circuits. Every thought pattern we generate within our mind uses neural connections. When we **repeatedly harbour a pattern of thoughts, their neural circuit becomes etched in the brain.**

This phenomenon called 'neuroplasticity' is the ability of the mind to reorganise itself by forming new neural connections in response to situations or changes in the environment. The consequence of neuroplasticity is that when a neural circuit becomes intensely engraved in the brain, the corresponding thought pattern comes more easily to the mind, thereby conditioning it.

The first to postulate the impact of habituation on human and animal behaviour was Ivan Pavlov, the famous Russian physiologist who won the Nobel Prize for Medicine in 1904. You may have heard of his famous experiments with dogs.

Pavlov's research paved the way for the 'classical conditioning' theory. He initially began his study to gather information on the digestive system of dogs. With the help of his laboratory assistants, he documented the amount dogs would salivate (since mammals produce saliva in the mouth that helps break down food). The lab assistants who fed the dogs would wear white coats.

However, Pavlov soon noticed that even without being presented with food, the dogs began drooling simply on seeing the white-coat assistants. He then conducted a study in which he rang a bell every time he fed the dogs. Soon, just ringing of the bell made the dogs salivate. The dogs had learned to associate the bell with the food, and as a result, ringing the bell evoked the same response as the food itself.

This led to the theory of 'classical conditioning' which shed new light on human behaviour. Psychologists now understood how thought patterns get etched in neural pathways in the brain.

How can we leverage this nature of neuroplasticity to our benefit? This requires us to first understand the process of habit formation.

The Physiology of Habit Formation

Whenever we decide to do any physical or mental work, our brain fires neurons in different regions including the sensory motor region, the neocortex, and the prefrontal lobes. But the beauty is that the brain has a self-programming ability. When it sees some activity being repeated, it creates shortcuts of the neural sequences and stores them in the basal ganglia, the part of the brain responsible for learning, habits, and emotions. This enables the brain to engage in those activities with greater ease in the future. Habit formation is thus the brain's way of simplifying its work and making it more efficient.

For example, the first time we began typing, our brain had to exert itself to the maximum to identify and press the required keys. Consequently, it took us a few minutes to type a handful of words. However, as we continued typing, the brain began programming itself. The moment we thought of a letter, our finger would fly on the keyboard to press the corresponding key. The brain had created programmes for the neural sequences to be fired for the task.

With repeated practice, the brain began forming programmes for entire words, enabling the keys to be pressed in multiple sequences. As a result, after a year of training, we were typing at speeds of fifty words a minute and above.

Without such a self-programming ability, typing would have been as laborious as it was on the first day. Then we would be unable to think of anything else while typing. Fortunately, the power of habits simplifies the brain's work, and along with typing, we are also able to think, imagine, and plan.

Similarly, we multitask while we drive. We speak to passengers, listen to audio talks, and plan the rest of our day. However, on the first day of driving, the tasks of simultaneously controlling the steering, accelerator, and brakes are so formidable that they take up all our attention. With continued practice, the brain keeps programming itself, creating habits out of these tasks. Finally, the day comes when we can simultaneously drive and engage in a spirited conversation without risk.

By creating habitual programmes, the brain gets its work done while expending much less energy. A study was conducted to observe cerebral activity in rats. The rats were left in a maze, at a distance from a chunk of cheese. They slowly sniffed their way to it. As the experiment was repeated, their brain began learning the pathways and they progressed more quickly to the cheese. After a month, on being left in the maze they could run towards the cheese. The instruments on their head showed that brain activity progressively reduced as the learning occurred.

The Habit Loop

A habit has three parts to it: 1) stimulus, 2) response, and 3) reward. The stimulus works like a trigger for the brain which then responds with the conditioned behaviour. That behaviour generates a reward which further reinforces the pattern for the future.

For example, if for a month, while watching TV, you drank tea regularly, it would grow into a habit. Now, whenever you sit before the TV, it acts as a trigger. The brain responds by creating the desire for tea. And when you drink the tea, the sensual gratification is the reward that reinforces the habit loop.

The brain is so smart that it does not need an external reward for reinforcement. It generates the feel-good chemicals—serotonin, endorphin, and dopamine—and sends them to the part of the brain that was engaged in the activity. These chemicals create the 'feel-good' sensation which is the reward.

Consider another example. Suppose that working on your assignment is drudgery for the brain, which seeks some diversion. When you hear the chime of a new email, you go to your inbox and check it. This provides a welcome distraction from work. The brain gets relief from the present drudgery and a slight pleasure from the content of the email. Plus, the feel-good chemicals created by the brain reinforce the habit loop. Now every time the email bell chimes, the mind generates an irresistible desire for reading it, which is hard to overcome. It has become a habit.

The patterns of habits become so strong that people find themselves helpless in changing them. Studies have shown that habits remain even after surgery is done on the brains of alcoholics. On the appearance of old cues, the cravings for rewards manifest again, waiting to exert their power on the mind.

Cues for habitual behaviour can be of infinite variety—a picture of ice cream, a certain place, a certain time of the day, or the company of a particular person. The routines they trigger can be a mere emotion that comes for milliseconds or a complex sequence of behaviours. The rewards vary—emotional payoff, chemical gratification, sensual pleasure, mental stimulation, or any combination of these.

Habits often enter our lives without our conscious permission. But they grow so strong that they shape our destiny far more than we realise. They cause our brain to latch onto them, to the exclusion of all else, including common sense. In this way, habits can be compared to a cable. Each day, we weave a thread of the cable. The singular thread seems too weak to hold us, however, when woven together, the cable is almost unbreakable.

But the good news is that habits can be changed. Social researchers conducted studies to understand why families increased their fast food consumption when a fast food outlet moved into their neighbourhood. They found that advertisements, picturesque billboards, and other allurements successfully created cues for triggering the habit loop for eating French fries. The pleasurable taste of fat, salt, and crispy fries provided the natural reward. Inadvertently, customer behaviour was influenced to the extent that some of the families began taking their dinner daily at the fast food joint.

When the outlet moved out of the neighbourhood, the family habit slowly began changing. They started having food at home more often. Within a year, the habit had fully subsided The conclusion was that habits are changeable.

The brain's quality of neuroplasticity works like a two-edged sword. On the negative side, it programmes and shackles our thinking in deleterious thought patterns. On the positive side, it provides an opportunity to reshape the brain, disband old habits, and install new ones. Thus, habits can be learned and unlearned. The potential is immense!

Good and Bad Habits

Habits can be compared to macros in an Excel sheet. If we have tasks we wish to repeat in multiple cells, we can record a macro to automate them and quickly apply the set of actions to selected cells. Habits are like macros in the brain. On receiving the given cue, the brain automatically performs the actions of its programming.

However, there is a catch to it. The created macro does not care whether it was correctly designed or not. If correct, it saves time through automated processes. But if the macro itself is wrong, we end up with a messed up excel sheet. Likewise, habits too programme the brain for our benefit or harm. Here is an anecdotal tale about habits.

In the early twentieth century, a British explorer came across a group of cannibals. They sat around a feast of human flesh and were about to eat. The explorer was surprised to learn that the tribal chief had studied at Cambridge University.

'You have received good education and you still eat human flesh?' the traveller asked.

'Yes,' replied the cannibal chief. 'The only difference is that earlier I used to eat with my fingers, and now I eat with a knife and fork.'

As the vintage saying goes, 'Old habits die hard.'

Unfortunately, good habits require effort for their creation, while bad habits develop all too easily. You indulge in something that gives pleasure in the moment. While the habit is forming, you do not realise the serious long-term harm it is causing, and you carelessly repeat the pleasurable indulgence. In a few weeks, the habit grips you, and you find yourself bound by the habit loop: stimulus—response—reward.

Good habits are hard to come by and easy to live with. Conversely, bad habits develop easily and are hard to live with. Given the fact that bad habits harm us, we need to be more aware of the repeated choices we make. Very often, people unconsciously make choices in their lives. It is like the horse rider, who, when asked where he was going, replied, 'I don't know, ask the horse.' The horse rider's response was comical because he should have set the direction, not the horse. Similarly, our unconscious choices create bad habits we later live to regret.

The reason bad habits get a grip on us is that the first few times we repeat a harmful behaviour, it does not seem to do much damage. The first few puffs of a cigarette do not forebode that cigarettes are addictive. The initial pegs of alcohol do not warn us of the obsessive compulsion that lies ahead.

Take the example of a giant Sequoia tree that lives for over 2,000 years and grows up to a height of 300 feet, the height of a 20-storey building. Yet, as you travel the Yosemite forest in California, you find a huge Sequoia lying on the ground. What happened to it?

It was born two millennia in the past and was thriving until a few decades ago. Then, a beetle came to live on it. The huge tree seemed to be in no danger from the little creature. But within a year, there were hundreds of beetles crawling on the tree.

In four years, the beetles had made gigantic colonies on the tree. They now had the upper hand and were invincible. During the fifth year, the giant tree, one of the biggest in the world, had been felled by the tiny beetles.

Similarly, when a person first takes *bhāng* (marijuana), the changes in the body and mind seem so minute that the user is almost unaware of them. But the habit loop has been set in motion. Every indulgence thereafter acts like a thread in the cable until the cable is so strong that it becomes an addiction. Even visits to the rehabilitation centre are of no use in breaking it.

The same is the case with good habits. In the short run, their benefits may seem imperceptible. Going for one session of yoga on Sunday may not make any noticeable difference to your health. However, if you consistently do yoga five to six days a week, and continue week after week, then in the space of a few years, you will definitely become a healthier person.

Taking a glass of water upon waking up one day may be of no significance. But if you habitually drink water first thing every morning, your digestive system will undoubtedly become better in a few years. Thus, the benefit of a good habit is the cumulative impact it has in the long run.

Use the Power of Habits to Build a Noble Character

Over time, our habits form or build our character. A virtuous character is the consequence of morally upright habits. For example, if we are truthful day after day, week after week, and year after year, it becomes installed within us as a habit. In this way, honesty does not come by itself; it is a habit we ingrain within ourselves. Once installed, the habit of honesty prevents us from wandering off course morally or ethically in our day-to-day behaviour.

Building a noble character requires the elimination of detrimental habits and installation of beneficial ones. Without success in this, we will remain fettered slaves of our mind and senses. Like a rudderless ship in a stormy ocean, we will continually be tossed around by the waves of maya that come in the form of anger, greed, desire, envy, and illusion. Ralph Waldo Emerson expressed this well when he said:

> Sow a thought, reap an action;
> sow an action, reap a habit;
> sow a habit, reap a character;
> sow a character, reap a destiny.

We must thus apply ourselves to the task of breaking our dysfunctional habits and developing beneficial ones. If this seems an arduous task, let us take encouragement from the fact that even animals change painful habits, as the story here illustrates.

India has many popular tales of the seventeenth century Mughal emperor, Akbar, and his wise and intelligent minister, Birbal. It is said that Akbar once asked Birbal if there was anyone in his kingdom who could train goats to resist green grass. Birbal replied that it was a small matter, and he needed just a month to get it done.

Birbal then took a goat to his home. Everyday he would place fresh green grass before the goat, but the moment it would try to eat the grass, he would whack the goat severely on the mouth with a stick. Finally, even the goat's tiny intellect learned that eating the grass was too painful and the reward was not worth its while.

After a month's training, Birbal brought the goat to Akbar's court. He announced to the king, 'Your Majesty, this goat is trained. It will not eat even the most succulent grass.'

Akbar asked his servants to bring fresh grass. He put the grass before the goat's nose. In the meantime, Birbal twirled the stick in his hand. The goat looked at the grass, then looked at the stick, and turned its head away. It had learned to resist eating grass by grasping the dreadful penalty.

This story reveals the basic nature of all creatures including humans. We all wish to avoid pain. On becoming aware of the painful consequences, even the unintelligent goat learned to break away from its natural tendency of eating grass. Likewise, we too must become aware of the miserable long-term consequences of bad habits. **If we can convince ourselves of the harm they cause us and the pain they inflict upon us, we will be able to break their gravitational pull.** But this is only half the story.

At this point, it becomes important to understand the two different kinds of happiness that exist.

Two Types of Happiness: Śhreya and Preya

The Vedas speak about two kinds of pleasure: *śhreya* and *preya*. Śhreya is that pleasure which seems bitter in the beginning but becomes very sweet in the long run. Preya is that pleasure which seems pleasant in the present but causes great pain later. The difference between them is akin to delayed gratification versus immediate gratification.

An example of śhreya is the eating of amla or the Indian gooseberry. Amla is a superfood that is very beneficial for health. Each amla has the vitamin C of ten oranges. However, children dislike it since it has a bitter taste. Parents in India encourage children to eat it, saying: *āmle kā khāyā aur baḍoṅ kā kahā, bād meṅ patā chaltā hai.* 'The benefits of both these—eating amla and following the advice of elders—are experienced in the future.'

Interestingly, within a couple of minutes of eating the amla, the bitter taste in the mouth transforms into sweetness. And the long-term benefits of consuming natural vitamin C are undoubtedly numerous. Śhreya happiness is of the same nature—it appears bitter in the short-term but is like nectar in the end. Preya is the opposite—it seems like ambrosia initially but proves to be poisonous in the end.

Regarding śhreya and preya, the *Kaṭhopaniṣhad* of the *Krishna Yajur Veda* states:

anyachchhreyo 'nyadutaiva preyaste
ubhe nānārthe puruṣhaṁ sinītaḥ
tayoḥ śhreya ādadānasya sādhu bhavati
hīyate 'rthādya u preyo vṛiṇīte
śhreyaśhcha preyaśhcha manuṣhyametastau
samparītya vivinakti dhīraḥ
śhreyo hi dhīro 'bhi preyaso vṛiṇīte
preyo mando yogakṣhemād vṛinīte (1.2.1–2)

'There are two paths—one, "beneficial" and the other, "pleasant". These two lead humans to very different ends. The pleasant is enjoyable in the beginning and ends in pain. The ignorant are snared to the pleasant and perish. But the wise are not deceived by its attractions. They choose the beneficial one and finally attain happiness.'

With the help of this understanding, we feel empowered to modify bad habits. First, we must repeatedly analyse and convince ourselves of the benefits that will accrue from changing negative habits. Second, we must reflect deeply on the pain that will be caused by not changing. We can enumerate all the pleasures and pains, benefits and harmful effects, advantages and disadvantages.

For example, if we wish to develop the habit of setting aside a half-hour every day for exercise, a possible analysis could be:

Happiness from cultivating the habit of exercising for 30 minutes daily:

1) Improved well-being
2) Continued youthfulness
3) Feeling of time well spent
4) More mental clarity
5) Improved self-image
6) Reduction of bad cholesterol
7) Development of a healthy heart
8) Improved muscle mass
9) More appealing personality
10) Greater stamina for work

Pain from not cultivating this healthy habit:

1) Unhealthy body
2) Lethargy
3) Weight gain
4) Forced to buy new clothes
5) Displeasure of spouse
6) Lack of self-confidence among friends
7) Earlier onset of old age
8) Increased risk of blood sugar and diabetes
9) Weak self-image
10) Lack of self-control and willpower

This is a sample analysis for developing a good habit. Now, if we wish to get rid of a bad habit, how should we convince ourselves? We can list the happiness we will get by eradicating it; we should also make a list of the pain if we continue with it.

For example, if we wish to break the habit of eating junk food, a possible analysis could be:

Happiness from breaking the habit of eating junk food

1) Weight control
2) Reduced risk of diabetes
3) Focus on more nutritious diet
4) Longer and healthier life
5) Improved self-image
6) The 'feel-good' factor of a better conscience
7) More appealing personality
8) Greater stamina for work
9) Financial savings
10) Spouse's satisfaction and respect

Pain from continuing the habit of eating junk food

1) Obesity
2) Displeasure of spouse
3) Lack of self-control and willpower
4) Discomfort of conscience for not doing what is proper
5) Poor self-image due to weak will
6) Disrespect of friends and well-wishers
7) Shorter and unhealthier life
8) Reduced energy for work
9) Early onset of old age
10) Increased risk of diabetes

We must deeply convince ourselves of the painful consequences of bad habits and the peace of mind that accrues from good habits. The technique of contemplation (*chintan*)—reflecting upon a piece of knowledge to transform it into a conviction—will be elaborated in the fifth chapter.

When we are deeply convinced about the benefits of a certain thought pattern or action, we naturally try to adopt it. It grows on us every time we practice it. With sufficient repetition, the new thought or behaviour solidifies into a new habit, replacing the old one. Then one day, like the firm rope made from puny blades of straw, the new behaviour becomes an integral part of our personality. This is how one develops a great personality, with a shining character forged from virtuous habits.

Jagadguru Kripalu-ji Maharaj recommended spending a few minutes for introspection before going to bed every day, to reflect on where we improved our behaviour and where we needed to put in more effort. He advised maintaining a diary for the purpose. **A diary or journal is a powerful tool for staying on track in the effort for self-improvement.**

Mahatma Gandhi was fond of maintaining a self-improvement diary. Benjamin Franklin is another famous example of someone who used a diary for establishing good habits. His efforts for self-transformation are chronicled in *The Autobiography of Benjamin Franklin.* He had a list of thirteen habits that he wanted to change. He jotted them down and then focused on one habit every week. He kept track of it daily—documenting whether he practised it or not; a simple check-mark (√) indicated success while a cross (x) indicated failure. At the end of the week, he could see how well he was adopting the habit of the week.

Breaking the Gravitational Pull of Bad Habits

The best time to overcome bad habits is before they are established. Our rational intellect must evaluate their cumulative power. Drinking a peg of alcohol may not be bad for health in a day, but over the years, ingesting hundreds of gallons will definitely be unhealthy for us. An action when done just once is negligible but becomes very significant when it is repeated over an extended period of time.

However, if bad habits have already been created, they do not go away on their own. They are always 'undo-it-yourself' projects. They are like cables formed from iron strands. Individually, the strands can be snapped with a little effort. But tied together, they become a formidable cable with the strength to lift many tons of weight. Likewise, stray actions are easy to correct, but once etched as habits by force of repetition, they possess strength that becomes difficult to break.

As a result, changing old habits is never easy. It is like launching a rocket into space. In the first few minutes of the flight as the rocket breaks through the downward pull of gravity, maximum fuel is needed. Once the escape velocity has been achieved, the energy consumed becomes marginal, and the rocket is practically propelled by its own momentum. Hence, more fuel is consumed in the lift-off than in the millions of miles of travel that follows.

I HAVE BEEN ADVISED TO CHANGE MY HABITS. SO I AM GIVING UP THE GOOD ONES. THEY'RE EASIER TO STOP THAN THE BAD ONES.

The same applies to habits. They exert a gravitational force on our personality that must be broken with patience, commitment, and understanding. The 'lift-off' demands tremendous effort. But once we break out of the gravitational pull of shackling habits, our freedom acquires a completely new dimension.

So, how can we achieve this 'lift-off'?

The Importance of Willpower

Changing habits can be a profitable task but also one of the most challenging. Uprooting bad habits that have grown up to become mighty oaks is no child's play. Even the slightest progress in this direction requires self-control—to resist bad behaviour and act upon the good one. Thus, we may read the best books and hear the best knowledge, but if we are lacking in willpower, we will not be able to benefit from this information.

The gap between knowledge and its practice must always be bridged by 'discipline'. Abundance of willpower provides us the strength to resist animal-like impulses when they raise their head. Hence, it is on the bedrock of self-restraint that we must build habits that will bestow on us a lifetime of courage, forbearance, and peace. In reality, lack of self-control is akin to a mental disease that makes us feeble and irresolute. When we see this weakness within, we must make it a priority to stamp it out.

We develop self-discipline by exercising it, in much the same way as we build our muscles. Every time we follow through on a resolution, we liberate the force of willpower within. But each time we break our resolve not to indulge in sense pleasures, the muscle of self-control becomes emaciated.

In this way, small moment-to-moment victories lead to larger successes. The more we exert our willpower, the greater it grows. But if we neglect it, our self-discipline will dwindle and wither away, like unused muscles in the body. Let us exert ourselves courageously to fight the gravitational pull of our bad habits. Once the new habit begins to grow, it becomes progressively easier, and then, one day the desired behaviour comes naturally.

When we see people with stellar qualities, we wonder how they reached there. Well, it was all a matter of exerting their willpower for some time, until the new habit kicked in. As simple as that. Understanding this, let us push ourselves to unleash the power of a controlled mind and an illumined intellect. I have covered this topic in great detail in my book, *7 Mindsets for Success, Happiness, and Fulfilment.*

Having said this, a word of caution is again necessary, for changing habits is never easy. Even when the change seems to have been effected, there is always a danger of falling back into old behaviours and thought patterns. The reason is that the basal ganglia remembers the context that triggers a habit, so old habits can be revived whenever triggers reappear. Thus it is important, while endeavouring to change, to warily avoid the triggers that previously reinforced the old habit.

With a firm decision to transform, we should exercise utmost care to sidestep the contexts conducive to old habits. Such a firm decision requires the intellect to become resolute and illumined. Our discussion on habits has naturally led to the topic of the intellect. What is its function and how is it different from the mind? We consider this question in the next chapter.

SUMMARY OF THE MAIN POINTS

- Most of our thoughts and behaviours are not a consciously analysed response to situations. We respond involuntarily based on our habitual thought patterns.
- Positive thinking cannot be accomplished through individual thoughts. It requires installing the desired thought patterns as habits within ourselves.
- A repetitive thought etches a deep groove in the neural network of the brain, making the recurrence of that thought very easy. In this manner, habits exert a gravitational pull upon our behaviour that becomes difficult to break.
- Good character is the result of good habits while bad character results from bad habits.
- To change unwanted habits, we must repeatedly convince ourselves of the benefits that will accrue from changing these detrimental habits. We must also reflect deeply about the pain that will be caused by not changing them
- Just as a rocket expended more fuel during take-off than in the rest of its flight, similarly the 'lift-off' in the process of forging new habits is the most difficult. It requires developing and exercising the muscle of willpower.
- With sufficient repetition, the new behaviour or thought develops into a new habit, replacing the old one.

  During the transition phase, avoid the context that triggers the old habit.

THE ROLE OF INTELLECT IN CONTROLLING THE MIND

We all are acquainted with our whimsical mind. It flits from place to place and from topic to topic like the ball in a roulette game. It wanders off even from very interesting topics, then what to say of its rebelliousness when the work at hand is dreary! Consequently, we develop the notion that our mind is not under our control and that we just have to put up with unwelcome distractions and thoughts. However, this is not the case. If we learn to harness the power of the intellect, we will discover immense ability to manage our mind.

In the last chapter, we learned how breaking bad habits and developing good ones requires a resolute intellect. The Bhagavad Gita also repeatedly refers to the importance of the intellect. In it, Lord Krishna describes His teachings as *Buddhi Yog* or the 'Yoga of the Intellect'. He repeatedly instructs Arjun to surrender his intellect to God. In light of this, let us explore the intellect's position in the internal hierarchy

How the Mind and Intellect Interact

The intellect makes decisions and the mind generates desires. For example, if the intellect decides that happiness is in ice creams, the mind hankers for it. If the intellect decides that money will solve all of life's problems, the mind thinks ... money, money, money. And if the intellect decides that prestige is the source of happiness, the mind yearns to be famous and respected in society. In other words, the intellect makes the decisions and the mind engages in *sankalp* (hankering) and *vikalp* (aversion). Between them, the intellect's position is of paramount importance.

An example will make this very clear.

Let us say Ganga Prasad has not eaten for four days. He is very tormented. Food ... food ... food ... is all he can think about. After four days, he is presented with a silver plate filled with delicious foods. His mouth salivates, and the senses hanker for relishing the contact with their sense objects. The mind asks the intellect for the go-ahead to pick up a delicious gulab jamun (an Indian dessert).

The intellect instructs the mind, 'Yes, yes go ahead; I am also very tormented. Do not delay! Pick it up.'

The mind instructs the hand, and it picks up the gulab jamun. The hand brings it up to his mouth. The senses are eager and the stomach rumbles. Will anything be able to change his mind at this moment? 'Impossible,' you may think.

But suddenly his friend cries out, 'What are you doing? Do you wish to die? That gulab jamun has been poisoned!'

'Poison? Die? Something is wrong here.' The intellect commands, 'Stop!' The intellect instructs the mind which instructs the hand. The hand tosses away the gulab jamun.

Now see if he will change his mind? Offer him a temptation: 'Sir, we will give you one crore to consume that gulab jamun. Please eat it.'

'What will I do with a crore, if I die? No, thank you.' He won't budge, no matter how hungry he is, for his intellect is convinced that eating the gulab jamun will kill him.

Ask him again, 'How do you know the food is poisoned?'

'My friend told me,' he replies.

'Is your friend perfectly honest? Is he an avatar of the truthful Harishchandra?'

'No, no, I have often caught him telling lies.'

'Okay, never mind. Have you ever seen poison in your life?'

'No.'

'So, you have never seen poison in your life, and yet one statement from this untrustworthy friend made you throw away the gulab jamun?'

'Yes.'

How did Ganga Prasad gain such control over the mind? Though he was hungry for the last four days and his senses were hankering for food, he abstained from the delicious gulab jamun.

The control came from the intellect. When it decided that the gulab jamun is harmful to his self-interest, it clamped down upon the mind and senses. The *Yajur Veda* states:

vijñāna sārathiryastu manaḥ pragrahavān naraḥ
so 'dhvanaḥ pāramāpnoti tadviṣhṇoḥ paraṁ padam

(*Kaṭhopaniṣhad* 1.3.9)

'To cross over the material ocean and attain your divine goal, **illumine your intellect with divine knowledge, then with the illumined intellect, control the unruly mind.'** This is why it is said, 'Knowledge is power!' for it is true or correct knowledge that enables good decision-making.

Usually, however, the situation is not so straightforward. The mind and intellect are not always in accord. Sometimes, the intellect is unclear about what is beneficial, and at other times, the mind is adamant about the object it craves. Thus, strife arises in the internal machinery. Let us understand our inner apparatus further.

The Four Aspects of Our Internal Machinery

The Vedic scriptures describe our *antah karan* (mind or ethereal heart) as having four aspects:

1) Mind (*mana*): It creates the thoughts, feelings, desires, hankerings, and aversions.
2) Intellect (*buddhi*): Its function is to analyse and decide. It understands, decides, and discriminates i.e. this is good this is bad.
3) Subconscious mind (*chitta*): It is the storehouse of impressions and memories. It enables one to get attached to an object or person.
4) Ego (*ahankār*): It is the ego or 'I'ness. It produces the sense of identity with the attributes of the body and creates pride.

These are not four separate entities, rather, they are simply four levels of functioning of the one mind. Hence, we may either refer to all of them together as the mind, or as the mind-intellect, or as the mind-intellect-ego, or as the mind-intellect-subconscious-ego mechanism. They all refer to the same thing.

Various scriptures designate the mind in any of these four ways:

1) *Mana*: The *Pañchadaśhī* refers to all four together as the mind, and states that it is the cause of material bondage.
2) *Mana-buddhi*: In the Bhagavad Gita, Shree Krishna repeatedly talks of the mind and the intellect as two things and emphasises the need to control both (and to surrender them to God).
3) *Mana-buddhi-ahankār*: The *Yog Darśhan* refers to the inner mechanism in terms of three entities—mind, intellect, and ego—that must be disciplined (to attain union with God).
4) *Mana-buddhi-chitta-ahankār*: Shankaracharya, while explaining the apparatus available to the soul, has classified the mind into four—mind, intellect, subconscious, and ego.

All the above designations refer to the same internal gear within us, which is together called antaḥ karaṇ. Among the four states of the mind, the two most important are the mana and the buddhi.

The Battle Between Mind and Intellect

We had discussed earlier that the intellect possesses the decision-making power. If it decides that eating a rasgulla (an Indian dessert) will give happiness, then the mind desires, 'I want a rasgulla for dinner today'. See, the intellect made the decision, and the mind followed by creating a corresponding desire for rasgulla. This is an instance where the intellect decides and the mind desires accordingly.

Consider another scenario. A thought arises: 'I am not eating well these days. Tonight, I will cook broccoli, cauliflower, and beans.' The intellect contemplates this and has a favourable evaluation. The mind rebels, and thinks, 'Yuck! Healthy food is so boring!' The mind now has a strong desire for something less healthy and tastier. 'How about a nice veggie burger and fries instead? Yum!'

In this way, the mind resists the intellect and presents a desire for junk food. But it is not what the intellect considers best for the health of the body. Now the battle is on between the mind's cravings and the intellect's knowledge. As a possible outcome, the intellect yields to the mind's desire for the veggie burger and even sanctions it. But is this a case of proper mind management? You know it isn't!

Controlling the mind requires us to empower the intellect with divine wisdom. Then, we use the intellect to govern the mind. Jagadguru Kripalu-ji Maharaj states:

mana ko māno śhatru usakī sunahu jani kachhu pyāre
(*Sadhana Karu Pyāre*)

'Dear one! Consider the impure mind to be your enemy. Do not listen to its whims.'

The desirous mind is like a little child. It wants immediate gratification of pleasure and the removal of pain. It is like the 'Id' in Sigmund Freud's psychoanalytic theory: 'I want what I

want, when I want, the way I want it, and I want it now!' We should not succumb to its tugging. Instead, we should use the discerning intellect to judge what is good and what is bad.

The Power of Discernment

The ability of the intellect to control the mind is called *vivek* (power of discernment). We all possess it and use it to varying degrees. But since we have not harnessed its full potential, we erroneously conclude that the mind is not under our control.

Here are some examples that highlight the power of the intellect in controlling the mind:

There are very few people who actually enjoy their professional work. Given the choice, instead of going to the office, they would much rather stay at home with their family. This is why most people feel joyful on Friday evenings at the thought of having two holidays ahead. Similarly, for many, Monday morning is a time for dejection, as the thought of five days of work ahead saddens the mind. This shows that the mind dislikes the drudgery of office. Yet, against the desires of the mind, even an ordinary person works at least eight hours a day.

What enables this subjugation of the mind? It is the power of the intellect. Once the intellect decides that work is necessary for living, it controls the mind. That is how the whole world manages to work, despite the complaining mind. Instead, if the mind was allowed to have its way, then staying in the office all day long would be impossible for most people.

Have you ever wondered why anger flows downward? The CEO shouts at the director. The director does not shout back because the intellect realises that it will cost him his job if he were to do so; instead, he vents his anger upon his manager. The manager controls himself, despite feeling vexed with the director, but finds release by shouting at the foreman. The foreman takes it all out at the worker. The worker purges his frustration on the wife. The wife shouts at the child. The child lets it out on the dog. In each case, the intellect decides where it is dangerous to get angry, and where it does not have repercussions. This proves that all of us, with the discernment of the intellect, can control our anger.

This capability of discernment, called vivek, is granted primarily to humans. The intellect of other species is not endowed with it beyond a marginal extent. They cannot think, 'Though my mind and senses are eager for food, I will observe a fast for spiritual purification.' But humans have been vested with the capacity for vivek, and they are expected to use it to rein in their mind and senses. **The moment we relinquish the intellect's power of discernment between right and wrong, we fall to the level of animals.**

The gift of receiving the human form comes with the responsibility of living by the wisdom of the intellect and not by the whims of the mind. Thus, the Vedas state:

tattva vismaraṇāt bhekivat

'One who abandons vivek (discernment) in one's actions becomes like a beast.'

Even children use discernment. Suppose, the parents are watching TV in the next room. The child is tempted to do the same, but then she thinks, 'I have my exam tomorrow. If I do not study, I will fail'. The child successfully uses her intellect to control the mind's desire for gratification.

Now consider a more powerful example. The parents of a child called Munna are anxious because he does not apply himself to studies. They ask him the reason for it. He responds by saying that his mind is unable to focus on studies—it keeps wandering in all directions. Munna and his parents are both worried by the problem which seems to have no solution.

Yet, when the same child goes for his year-end final exam, he brings his mind under control and totally focuses on answering the question paper for three hours. When the time is up, the examiner has to snatch the answer sheet out of his hands. But for those three hours, he did not get distracted by anything.

How did he garner such concentration, when all year round, he was complaining about his mind's inability to focus on his lessons? This became possible by the decision of the intellect. When his intellect decided that those three hours were important, and carelessness would result in loss of the entire year, it forced the mind to apply itself.

If that level of concentration had been maintained throughout the year, Munna would have stood a good chance of becoming a national level scholar. However, throughout the year, his intellect's decision was, 'Studies are not important. They are important for my parents, but they do not know anything. They do not understand that playing cricket with my friends is far more important.'

When the decision of the intellect was otherwise, there was no scope for the mind to remain focused. Even if it did get focused for a few moments, the intellect would jerk it away, 'There is no happiness here. Think of cricket; that is where true pleasure lies.'

This example illustrates the power of the intellect in controlling the mind. We must, therefore, cultivate it with correct knowledge and use it to guide the mind in the proper direction. If our intellect has mistaken values and insufficient knowledge, where will our life end up?

The science of mind management requires us to empower the intellect with right knowledge from the scriptures and then use that illumined intellect to properly govern the mind.

The Yoga of the Intellect

In the Bhagavad Gita, the science of mind management is repeatedly referred to as Buddhi Yog (Yoga of the Intellect):

buddhi-yogam upāśhritya mach-chittaḥ satataṁ bhava
(18.57)

'Taking shelter of buddhi yog, keep your consciousness always absorbed in Me.'

Who will perform the yoga of the intellect? The soul. What is this soul? The Vedic scriptures state that we are the soul situated within the body in the region of the heart. We are not our thoughts or actions; we are not what belongs to us. Our soul, and not the impermanent body, is the essence of who we are. And the soul is a tiny part of God.

To enable us to comprehend the positional role of the soul in the body, the Vedas give the analogy of a chariot:

ātmānaṁ rathinaṁ viddhi śharīraṁ ratham eva tu
buddhiṁ tu sārathiṁ viddhi manaḥ pragraham eva cha
indriyāṇi hayān āhur viṣhayāṁs teṣhu gocharān
ātmendriya-mano-yuktaṁ bhoktety āhur manīṣhiṇaḥ
(*Kaṭhopaniṣhad* 1.3.3-4)

The Upanishads say there is a chariot that has five horses pulling it; the horses have reins in their mouths; the reins are in the hands of the charioteer; a passenger is sitting at the back of the chariot. In this analogy:

- the chariot is the body
- the horses are the five senses

- the reins in the mouth of the horses is the mind
- the charioteer is the intellect
- the passenger seated behind is the soul

Ideally, the passenger should give directions to the charioteer, who should pull the reins to guide the horses in the proper direction. In the same way, the soul should direct the intellect, which should govern the mind. Then the mind should control the senses. But in this case, the soul (passenger) is asleep, and the chariot is going awry:

- the senses (horses) desire to see, taste, touch, feel, and smell various things
- the mind (reins), rather than controlling the senses, supports their desires
- the intellect (charioteer), instead of directing where to go, submits to the pulls of the senses
- seated on this chariot, the soul (passenger) is moving around in this material world since eternity

We are like the passenger, asleep in the chariot, who has relinquished control. As a result, the driver of the chariot (the intellect) has no clue in which direction it should go. The soul (passenger) needs to wake up and become proactive. It can then steer the intellect in the right direction.

Thus, it is important to illumine the intellect with perfect, flawless knowledge. For this, we need to find a perfect source of knowledge. What is that source?

Theoretical Knowledge vs Realised Wisdom

There are two kinds of knowledge—theoretical knowledge and practical realisation.

For example, let us say that a lady has memorised all the recipes in her cookbook but has never even entered the kitchen in all her life. Undoubtedly, she possesses theoretical knowledge of cooking. Another woman has been cooking for the last sixty years and has experienced all of its intricacies. She possesses practical knowledge of cooking. Such knowledge is far superior to mere bookish knowledge.

Similarly, in spirituality, theoretical knowledge is that where one has read, or even memorised the books of wisdom, but has never done sadhana. Bookish wisdom is not accompanied by inner realisation since the mind is yet impure.

On the other hand, as the mind gets purified, sublime knowledge begins to emerge from within. This is the inner realisation, which is far more valuable than all the books of knowledge in the world. The dawning of inner wisdom is true knowledge that dispels the darkness of ignorance within us.

However, to experience the emergence of inner wisdom, we need to understand theoretical knowledge as well. Only then can we identify and appreciate the process of self-purification and implement it in our life. **Thus, theoretical knowledge is not the goal; yet, it is necessary if we wish to purify the mind and experience inner realisation.**

Let us now understand from where and how we can acquire the theoretical knowledge of spirituality and its tools.

Ascending and Descending Processes of Learning

There are two ways of acquiring theoretical knowledge. The first is the ascending process in which we use our senses, mind, and intellect to explore, discover, and conclude about the nature of truth. The second is the descending process where we simply receive the knowledge from a proper source. The ascending process of gaining knowledge is inherently prone to defects. Since our senses, mind, and intellect are made from material energy, they are imperfect and limited. Therefore, we can never be completely sure about the accuracy and reliability of the knowledge we gain through them.

As the pursuit of material science is based upon the ascending process, even the most acclaimed scientific theories of the past are overthrown and superseded by newer ones. For example, the Greek concept of matter as indivisible atoms was invalidated by Ernest Rutherford when he demonstrated that atoms consist of electrons, protons, neutrons, and vast regions of empty space. Rutherford's theory was later overthrown by

the Quantum theory, which stated that electrons and protons are not solid particles, but vibrating patterns of energy with a dual particle-wave nature. This makes us wonder whether the beliefs we hold today will be overthrown by new theories after a few centuries.

On the other hand, the descending process of gaining knowledge is completely devoid of such defects. When we receive knowledge from a perfect source, we can be assured that it is flawless. For example, if we wish to know who our father is, we do not conduct experiments. We simply ask our mother as she is the authority on this piece of information. Likewise, in spiritual matters too, the descending process immediately gives us access to vast reservoirs of knowledge which would have otherwise taken ages of self-effort to unveil. **The only criterion here is that the source from which we receive the knowledge must be infallible and trustworthy.** The Vedas are such a source of knowledge.

The Vedas are not the name of any book. They refer to the eternal knowledge of God, which He manifests every time He creates the world. In the present cycle of creation, God first revealed them in the heart of the first-born Brahma. These Vedas were then passed on for ages by oral tradition, from master to disciple, and hence another name for them is *shruti* (knowledge received by hearing). They are also called *apauruṣheya* (not created by any human). For this reason, in Indian philosophy, the Vedas are considered the ultimate authority for validating any spiritual principle.

bhūtaṁ bhavyaṁ bhaviṣhyaṁ cha sarvaṁ vedāt prasidhyati

'The veracity of any spiritual principle must be authenticated on the authority of the Vedas.' The four Vedas are: *Rig Veda, Yajur Veda, Sama Veda,* and *Atharva Veda.*

To elaborate the meaning of the Vedas further, many more scriptures have been written. These scriptures do not deviate from the authority of the Vedas, rather they attempt to expand and explain the knowledge contained in them. Together, all these are termed as 'Vedic scriptures'.

These Vedic scriptures are the source from where we can acquire perfect knowledge. They are understood through the guru—the enlightened saint who has practically realised their wisdom. In this process, someone who is a perfect authority on the knowledge passes it down to another who wishes to know. If we wish to verify the knowledge we receive from our guru, we can compare it with that from all the other God-realised saints in history. They can be referred to as *saḍhus* (saints). Thus, when guru (our spiritual master), sadhu (other God-realised saints), and *Śhāstras* (Vedic scriptures) confirm the same spiritual principle, we can be assured that the knowledge is infallible and perfect. This is the descending process of learning.

In contrast is the ascending process of learning, where one endeavours to enhance the frontiers of understanding through self-effort. The ascending process is laborious, imperfect, and time-consuming. For example, if we wish to learn physics, we could eithe. try to do it by the ascending process where we speculate about its principles with our own intellect and then reach conclusions, or we could do it by the descending process where we approach a good teacher of the subject. The ascending process is exceedingly time-consuming, and we may not even be able to complete the inquiry in our lifetime. We can also not be sure about the validity of our conclusions.

In comparison, the descending process gives us instant access to the deepest secrets of physics. If our teacher has perfect knowledge of physics, then it is very straightforward—simply listen to the science from the educator and digest what is said. This descending process of receiving knowledge is both easy and faultless.

Every year, thousands of self-help books are released in the market which present authors' solutions to the problems encountered in life. These books may be helpful in a limited way, but because they are based upon the ascending process of attaining knowledge, they are imperfect. Every few years, a new theory comes along that overthrows the current ones.

On the other hand, divine knowledge does not need to be created by self-effort. It is an energy of God, and has existed ever since He has existed, just as heat and light are as old as the fire from which they emanate. An amazing endorsement of this truism is the Bhagavad Gita itself, which continues to astound people with its perennial wisdom that remains relevant to our daily lives even fifty centuries after it was spoken.

The principles revealed in this book are not a new discovery. They are only elaborations of the eternal truths of the Vedas. Hence, I have quoted the relevant Vedic mantras, verses, and aphorisms at appropriate places to authenticate the knowledge presented. I received these secrets of Vedic knowledge from a true guru, Jagadguru Shree Kripalu-ji Maharaj, who was the fifth original Jagadguru of Indian history.

The next question that arises is how can we transform the pearls of divine wisdom from theory to practice and thereby close the gap between our knowledge and its implementation? This requires the three-fold process of *śhravaṇ* (hearing divine knowledge), *manan* (contemplation upon the divine knowledge), and *nididhyāsan* (resolution of the intellect). We will learn about them in the next chapter.

SUMMARY OF THE MAIN POINTS

» In our inner machinery, the intellect decides whether something is use ful or harmful to us, and whether it will give happiness or pain. The mind harbours the desire or aversion for the object, person, or circumstance.

» God has endowed the human intellect with the ability to control the mind. This ability is called vivek. However, the mind is like a spoiled child that wants immediate gratification. This invariably leads to a fight between the intellect and the mind.

» To rein in the mind, the intellect must exercise its ability for discernment. In the Bhagavad Gita, this is called Buddhi Yog. discernment requires empowering the inttellect with divine knowledge.

» The ascending process of knowledge is long and tedious. Besides, one can never be sure about the reliability and validity of this knowledge.

- The descending process immediately places perfect and reliable knowledge at our disposal. The only requirement is that the source of knowledge be trustworthy.
- The Vedas are such a trustworthy source of knowledge. They are the knowledge that was revealed by God, and hence are called apaurusheya. They can only be understood through a guru, the enlightened saint, who has practically realised their wisdom.

THREE STEPS TO EMPOWER THE INTELLECT

In the preceding chapter, we compared the senses-mind-intellect mechanism to a chariot. The intellect is like the chariot driver, the mind the reins, and the senses are akin to horses. The intellect needs to be enriched with proper knowledge. The empowered intellect must then use the mind to rein in the senses.

Consider the example of a knife that is used to cut garlic. Since garlic is so strongly odorous, its smell sticks to the knife. Subsequently, whatever else we cut with the knife also smells of garlic. Similarly, if the intellect is wise and unbiased, it will guide the chariot in the proper direction. But, if the intellect itself is attached to mundane delights of the mind and senses, it will not possess the discernment required to make wise decisions.

The natural question that flows from this analogy is: How can we empower the intellect with divine wisdom, so that it may control the mind with razor-sharp discernment? This involves the three-fold process of śhravaṇ, manan, and nididhyāsan. Let us look at these steps, one at a time.

Śhravaṇ (Hearing Divine Knowledge)

To hear or read divine knowledge is śhravaṇ. As śhravaṇ opens our mind to the wisdom of the scriptures, it is naturally the first step in developing the wisdom of the intellect. Reading or hearing from the proper sources equips us with the perfect knowledge required for leading a successful life. Śhravaṇ has been greatly extolled in the Vedic scriptures.

In the Shreemad Bhagavatam, Emperor Parikshit asked his guru how the heart could be cleansed of impurities like anger, greed, hatred, and envy. Shukadev Paramahansa replied:

śhṛiṇvatāṁ swakathāṁ kṛiṣhṇaḥ puṇya śhravaṇa kīrtanaḥ
hṛidyantaḥ stho hyabhadrāṇi vidhunoti suhṛit satām
(1.2.17)

'O Parikshit, the Supreme Lord Shree Krishna is sitting in the heart of all living entities. He naturally cleans the minds of those who develop love for hearing His glories from the mouth of a saint.' Similarly, Saint Tulsidas has written:

eka ghaḍī ādhi ghaḍī, ādhi meṅ puni ādha
tūlasī saṅgata sādhu kī, koṭi kaṭe aparādha

'Listening to divine knowledge from saints is so powerful that even a brief moment of it is sufficient to destroy the karmic reactions of countless sins.'

To highlight the importance of hearing, Jagadguru Kripalu-ji Maharaj has composed a *pada* (hymn) titled: *Suno mana, eka kāma kī bāta* (*Prem Ras Madira*). Speaking to the mind, Maharaj-ji says: 'O my mind, listen now to a useful piece of knowledge. You have heard lots of things—this person got married, that person filed for divorce, a fire raged in this city, a tornado struck that city—but you have never heard anything useful. If you had, your work would have been done, and you would have attained your supreme destination. But the fact that you are still under the influence of maya proves that, as yet, you have not heard anything worthwhile.'

Kripalu-ji Maharaj's statement may appear to be very harsh at face value and raise eyebrows. People could refute it by saying, 'We have heard so many lectures. We attend the satsang of saints who visit our town. We even watch Maharaj-ji's lectures on TV and YouTube. In all these, we get good wisdom. How can Maharaj-ji say that we have not heard anything useful until now?'

There is no denying that **we did listen to divine teachings in the past. The problem is that we failed to implement what we heard.** As a result, the knowledge did not benefit us. Knowledge is only beneficial when it is applied, otherwise, it is worthless. We may know that there is poison in a cup, but if we insist on drinking it, then our knowledge is worthless. We may know the road to our destination, and yet, if we continue to go down the wrong road, our knowledge is of no value. Likewise, the ancient saying goes:

pustakasthā tu yā vidyā, parahasta gataṁ dhanaṁ
kāryakāle samutpanne na sā vidyā na taddhanaṁ

'The knowledge that we claim to possess, but which is still in our books, and the money that we count as our wealth, but which is in the hands of others, at the time of need, neither are of any use.' A hilarious story below illustrates this point.

A police officer was asleep in his home with his wife. Around midnight, a startling sound broke the wife's slumber. She shook her husband and with an alarmed voice said, 'My dear, can you hear the sound? It seems like some burglars are breaking into our house.'

The husband got up with a start and said, 'I know what that sound means. I can easily deduce that burglars are breaking into our home.'

After a couple of minutes, she said, 'It seems that they are now jumping into our drawing room from the window.'

'Yes, I am aware of what is happening,' replied the police officer. 'Nothing is hidden from me.'

A few moments later, the wife again said, 'They now seem to be pillaging goods from our cupboard.'

The police officer responded, 'I can infer it as clear as daylight. They are pillaging goods from our cupboard.'

After a while, the wife again cried in panic, 'My dear husband, they now appear to be running away with our things.'

'I know it all!' exclaimed the husband. 'They are fleeing with our things.'

'You know it all?' shrieked the poor lady. 'What is the use of knowing if you don't do anything??? You are a policeman. You have been trained in crime prevention drills. Go out and chase them. Recover our goods!!!'

The moral of the story is that knowledge is of no benefit unless we act upon it.

I AM EATING MORE HEALTHY NOW. MY SALAD IS MADE OF FRENCH FRIES, PAKORAS AND KACHORIS

And this is precisely where we lost out in the past. Though we received a lot of knowledge from discourses and satsangs, we did not bother to apply it. It went in from one ear and out from the other. Or even if we did implement the knowledge, it was only partially done. One per cent. Or ten per cent. Or twenty per cent. Or even ninety-nine per cent. But never a full one hundred per cent. And unless we implement it one hundred per cent and bring our thoughts and behaviour to the level of the faultlessness demanded by the scriptures, we will not attain the divine bliss of God that our soul seeks. The Bhagavad Gita says: *mām ekaṁ śharaṇaṁ vraja* (18.66). 'For divine grace to intercede and liberate us from material bondage, the surrender must be complete.'

This is why we are advised: *āvṛitti rasa kṛitupadeṣhāt.* Hear the message of the scriptures again. After that? Hear the message yet again. Then? Hear it once again.

But someone may complain: 'I am bored. I have already heard this knowledge before. Can I hear something else instead?'

'No, you will have to hear it again.'

'Why? Is there some compulsion?'

'Yes, there is a compulsion—it is the compulsion of your own soul.'

In this matter, there is no option. Until we experience the infinite bliss of God, our soul will never be satisfied. No matter what happiness we offer to it through the senses, mind, and intellect, our soul will still complain, 'This is not my bliss. Give me the divine bliss of my Lord'.

Hence, the Vedic texts instruct us to repeatedly hear divine teachings from the saints and the scriptures. This is the first stage of implementing the wisdom of the scriptures in our lives—śhravaṇ, meaning hearing or reading. Then comes the next stage, which is manan.

Manan (Contemplation)

After hearing, the next step is to retain the wisdom with us. **If we forget knowledge when we most need it, its benefits will escape us.** For example, we may know that anger is a bad thing, but when maya strikes us, we make the mistake of forgetting this important learning. Later, we regret, 'What did I do? I became livid on him who is like a father to me and thirty years my senior. What happened to me?' What happened was this: the knowledge that anger is a bad thing slipped away from the intellect, and the mistake was made.

Once a lady came up to me and said, 'Swami-ji, everything is all right with me, but I have one serious problem. I become angry very easily. Can you please give me some gems of wisdom that will help me conquer anger?'

I replied, 'Devi-ji, if I gave you a pin and asked you to puncture your arm with it, would you do so?'

'Of course not,' she replied. 'Why would I hurt myself with the pin?'

'Similarly,' I said, 'Anger hurts you first and foremost. You become angry at others thinking that you will teach them a lesson, but it is your own mind that harbours furious thoughts. This dirties your mind, poisons your blood, and weakens your heart. Therefore, knowing the harm it causes, why allow yourself to become angry?'

'That is a beautiful gem of wisdom,' the lady replied.

'Yes, but it will be of no use to you,' I said, 'Because when the attack of anger arises, this wisdom will slip out of your mind and you will make the mistake of losing your temper. Later, you will regret what you did.'

Hence, for knowledge to be implemented, it must always remain with us. And this requires internalising it through contemplation. **This is called manan, which means repeatedly**

revising the knowledge within our mind. While preparing for their exams, students revise their lessons repeatedly until they are memorised, and the knowledge is retained. Why do they work so hard on the knowledge? Because they realise its importance—every mark gained can make a difference to their career.

The same internal revision is necessary for spiritual knowledge as well. However, in spiritual matters we tend to become careless. 'I have heard it,' we say. Yes, we have heard it, but that is insufficient. We have to repeatedly contemplate on it, until it sinks into our consciousness and remains with us at the time of need.

There is a beautiful story illustrating the astonishing difference that forgetfulness of knowledge and its remembrance can make.

Raja Bhoj was a famous Rajput king in medieval India, who ruled over the kingdom of Malwa in the eleventh century. In his kingdom was a very learned pandit (priest). In his youth, the pandit had been an erudite scholar of the Vedic scriptures. However, when he grew old, he became poor, and the hardships he encountered destroyed his intellect. He needed money to maintain his family, home, and get his daughters married. He decided that the only option for him now was to steal. Where should he steal from? He deliberated that the best place would be the palace of Raja Bhoj himself.

With that intention, he walked to the king's palace. It was daytime and there were a lot of people walking in and out of the main gate. He mingled with them and inconspicuously entered the court. At night, when the courtiers began retiring for the day, he hid behind a piece of furniture.

In a little while, the court was deserted. Pandit-ji thought to himself, 'Let me begin stealing now.' He searched for the treasure room and with a stroke of luck, found it quickly. Seeing gold biscuits, he reached out to pick up some. But alas! The knowledge of the scriptures came streaming to his mind and he thought, 'I had read in the Garuḍ Purāṇ *that stealing gold is one of the* pañcha mahāpāp *(five deadly sins). If I do it, I will go to* Kumbhīpāk Narak *(one of the many hellish abodes described in the Puranas) and I definitely do not want such a consequence.'*

'Never mind,' he thought, 'If I cannot steal gold, let me steal diamonds.' He discovered where the royal diamonds were kept. He stooped forward to lift them, but the knowledge of the scriptures again came rushing to him. 'I had also read that stealing diamonds is a terrible crime and one who does it is sent to Raurav Narak *(another hellish abode). That will be too painful; I cannot do it.'*

Forgetting scriptural knowledge, pandit-ji had gone to steal. But each time he endeavoured to do so, the knowledge kept coming back to him. Whatever he would pick up, the scriptures would speak to him and restrain him. In this way, he kept moving things forward and backward for a while. He then concluded that stealing was not his cup of tea and decided to get out of the palace. But when he tried escaping, he discovered that there was a strong legion of guards at the gate. Raja Bhoj was a powerful king and his security arrangements were equally strong.

Pandit-ji concluded that there was no way of walking out of the palace at present. He decided to spend the night inside, and when more people would be around during the day, he would mingle with the crowd and walk out. But where could he spend the night, hidden from the guards? He thought that the safest place would be the bedroom of the king himself, for no one would look there. He walked into the king's bedroom and saw the king blissfully asleep on his bed. The pandit lay on the floor, under the king's bed, and fell asleep.

In the morning, a ceremony would take place to wake up the king. Brahmins would chant Vedic mantras, musicians would play on their instruments, women would dance, and elephants would blow their trumpets. The procedure commenced and Raja Bhoj started gliding from the dream state to the waking state. He sat up, stretched his arms, and yawned. Suddenly, a thought came to him: 'I am so fortunate; my treasure chests are full; I have such a huge army, with so many elephants and horses; these women are dancing for my pleasure; the Brahmins are reciting Vedic mantras for my sake.'

Raja Bhoj was a great patron of scholars. The great poet of Sanskrit literature, Mahakavi Kalidas, used to sit in his court. Through his association with Kalidas, the king had become quite a scholar himself. He began composing a verse. He composed and recited three lines of a verse, describing his good fortune on possessing such opulence:

cheto harā yuvatayaḥ suhṛidonukūlaḥ
sadbandhavāḥ praṇayagarbha giraśhcha bhṛityā
valganti danti nivahās taralās turaṅga ...

'Lovely women who steal the heart, friends who are favourably disposed, good relatives, servants who serve with submissive words, galloping horses, elephants that carry comfortably ...'

However, the fourth line did not come to him. He recited the first three lines again and again, but repeatedly got stuck at the fourth line.

Now pandit-ji was lying under the bed, listening to what the King was saying. In his mind, he was thinking the king is rejoicing in temporary things, for upon death, they will all be snatched away. The king made yet another attempt to complete the verse but was stuck once again. This time, pandit-ji could not resist. He blurted out:

sammīlane nayanayor nahi kiñchidasti

'None of these will remain once the eyes are closed (at death).'

Hearing those words, the king was startled out of his wits. 'Where did this voice come from?' he wondered. 'I am the only person in the room. And the message is so meaningful. Nothing will go with me after death.' The king concluded that this was a serious matter requiring further inspection. He called for his servants and asked them to investigate where the voice had come from.

Poor pandit-ji realised that he would be discovered in what he had thought was the safest haven in the palace. Rather than be dragged out unceremoniously, he decided to reveal himself. From under the bed, he poked his head out. The king saw him and exclaimed, 'Who are you, and what are you doing here?'

The pandit explained, 'O king, I am a renowned scholar of your kingdom, but poverty destroyed my intellect and I came to your palace to steal. However, each time I thought of picking something, the knowledge of the scriptures came rushing to me and I was unable to steal. That is why I came and hid here under your bed, so that I could slip away in the morning.'

The king replied, 'You are a very truthful person. I forgive you for your offence. But the line you have added is very special. "Nothing will go with me at the time of death." This line has opened my eyes. Why should I revel in the temporary treasures of the world? I have now developed detachment from worldly opulence. You are like my guru.' The king rewarded the pandit profusely and bid him farewell.

The story dramatically reveals the difference that recollection of knowledge makes. When the pandit forgot the teachings of the scriptures, he fell to the level of a thief. Later, when he recalled the same knowledge, he was unable to steal. Therefore, in order to implement what we have learned from the saints and scriptures, it is important to keep their teachings with us at all times. This is accomplished through manan which means revising the knowledge in our intellect.

When we contemplate on something, we think deeply about it. In today's culture, wherever we might live, we find less and less contemplative thinking. Newspapers and television news give us snippets rather than an in-depth exploration of a topic. Opinions that are stark and sensational are highlighted rather than the well-rounded ones. The political sphere is more about invective and rhetoric than thoughtful debate. All this reflects a deficiency of contemplation.

How then should we contemplate? Think of the cows masticating grass. They graze in the pasture for a portion of the day, and later, they sit and chew the grass for long hours.

Cows have four compartments in their stomach. They take their food out of one compartment, chew it finer, and then put it in the next one. In the same way, when we attend satsang, we hear divine teachings from the saints for an hour. Then, to get the most out of that knowledge, we must repeatedly ruminate over what we heard. The more we reflect upon it, the deeper it will sink inside.

What a person focuses his or her attention on, and contemplates upon, grows in life. The student who likes to solve puzzles and explore how things work is drawn towards engineering, science, or mathematics. The teenager who regularly thinks about trade, commerce, and how to make money is likely to become a banker or a stockbroker. Similarly, whatever knowledge we deliberate upon, grows within us.

Negative Chintan Devastates, While Positive Chintan Elevates

Contemplation is called manan in Sanskrit. Another word for it is chintan, which means the repetition of a thought, idea, or piece of knowledge, in the mind and intellect. It is a very powerful technique for mind management that can be used either for our benefit or loss, so much so that negative chintan can lead one to the point of suicide.

Let us say that a student fails her school final exam. She begins contemplating: 'I have failed. Now how will I show my face to my parents? What will they tell their friends? What will my friends say? I will be left behind in the same class while all the others will go to college. Life is too terrible. I cannot live anymore.' The consequence of such a chain of thoughts is that the student decides to end her life. Some of her classmates had also failed, but they bravely faced the difficult situation. They wondered what led their friend to commit suicide.

The problem was that she began negative contemplation which grew into a downward spiral as neural pathways got etched rapidly. Soon, she experienced that her contemplation was out of control. The chain of thoughts became so strong that it blew out of proportion and she felt totally helpless. This is the devastating power of negative chintan.

On the other hand, positive chintan has the potential to burn the impurities in our heart and develop sublime virtues. Let us say the same student who had committed suicide, had instead begun positive chintan: 'I was careless and lazy and I have paid the price for it. I must take this as a lesson and never make the same mistake again. I am so fortunate to have received such nice parents and to study in such a good school. I must not let my well-wishers down. I take a vow that from this moment, I will put in my best efforts to make them proud of me next year.'

What do you think would be the effect of such chintan on the student? If that thought process was deep and sufficient, it could transform her from being a failure to becoming an elite performer. That is how powerful contemplation is. **Negative chintan can devastate us, while positive chintan can lead us to perfection.**

Wherever people uplifted or degraded their minds, they leveraged the power of chintan. It was good chintan that made one soul into a saint like Prahlad, and it was bad chintan that made another soul into a demon like Emperor Hiranyakashipu (Prahlad's father).

The science of mind management requires transforming ourselves through beneficial chintan. Whenever we come across a gem of knowledge, whether in this book or elsewhere, we should note it down for permanency in our spiritual diary. Then we should contemplate on it deeply and repeatedly. **Even one piece of knowledge, if sufficiently reflected upon, has the power to transform us eternally.**

The beautiful thing about chintan is that it does not require any external resources. The amount of chintan we do depends

on us alone. Often, in worldly matters, we do an extreme amount of chintan. If a close relative insults us, we keep thinking about it until resentment consumes a significant portion of our thoughts. In comparison, when we hear divine knowledge from the saints, we are careless in reviewing it because we do not accord it much importance. Consequently, the knowledge slips out of our intellect and what we heard fails to get transformed into action.

Thus, in the Bhagavad Gita, Lord Krishna said to Arjun:

janma-mṛityu-jarā-vyādhi-duḥkha-doṣhānudarśhanam
(13.9)

'Repeatedly contemplate on the defects of material existence—birth, disease, old-age, and death.' This chintan will detach the mind from the world.

Of course, there were elevated personalities like the Buddha who did not need to do chintan. They were exposed to the knowledge once and were able to implement it right away. For example, all it took the Buddha to become detached was to see one sick person, one old person, and one dead person—once. That's it—just once. And he renounced the world.

But we are not at the level of the Buddha. Our intellect does not have that kind of grasping power, so we need to do chintan i.e. ruminate deeply on the knowledge. This chintan, also called manan, is the second step in empowering our intellect with divine wisdom.

After manan, comes the third step, nididhyāsan, which is explained below.

Nididhyāsan (Resolve Firmly with the Intellect)

Nididhyāsan is the third and final step in internalising knowledge. It means developing a firm decision of the intellect based upon this knowledge. In nididhyāsan, the knowledge turns into belief. The intellect says, 'This is it.'

What are beliefs? Every day, we make thousands of decisions about things that are either harmful or beneficial to us. It is impossible to empirically verify each decision we take. Beliefs are the convictions of our intellect regarding things to be true or false, without the need for empirical verification.

Beliefs decide our attitude towards people, objects, and situations. For example, we may believe that everyone is intrinsically good or we may believe that people are out to cheat us; we may believe that our situation is hopeless or we may believe that there is a silver lining to every cloud.

The world is full of innumerable stimuli. Our beliefs help us understand it simply. For example, we may believe that all religions contain some goodness and inspiration, or we may believe that all religions are hogwash. We will then look upon religious people and devotional practices accordingly. **Beliefs forge our worldview itself. They are the lens through which we understand and perceive the world.**

Beliefs dictate the importance we accord to things. Thus, based upon beliefs, we create our personal value system. If a person believes that hard work, dedication, and sincerity are always rewarded, she will develop her personal value system that accords great importance to diligence. If another person believes that people with the ability to dupe others get ahead in life, he will develop a value system that holds cheating and fraud as perfectly admirable means of work. **Either way, beliefs determine the direction of our life.** The Bible puts it very nicely:

> We walk by faith and not by sight. (2 Corinthians 5:7)

Mahatma Gandhi believed that satya (truthfulness) and ahimsa (non-violence) would triumph. His faith was so strong that he refused to budge from these tenets while opposing an empire that ruled half the world. Consequently, he launched a movement that was unprecedented in human history and led an entire nation to independence without the use of violence. His unflinching belief in the strength of truthfulness and non-

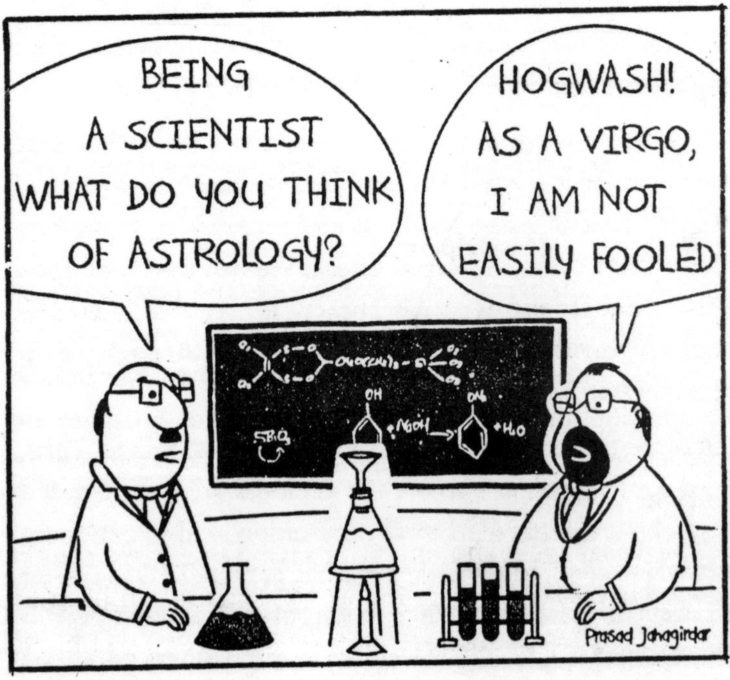

violence led to his unshakable values. Similarly, all our values such as hard work, sacrifice, discipline, loyalty, equality, and conservation of the environment, among others, originate from our beliefs.

The unsettling fact is that, invariably, we do not examine what we believe and why. By default, beliefs happen to us—they are acquired through family, society, dogma, or culture, without deep thought. For example, if we were cheated by two construction contractors in a row, based on our limited experience, we could conclude that all contractors must be cheats. It may be a far cry from reality, but we have now developed an internal conviction about contractors.

Likewise, if while growing up, our circle of friends believed that avant-garde pursuits were a sign of smartness, we may have imbibed the same belief without examining it. Many of our beliefs are unproductive, and some are even destructive, but we create attitudes and values based on them.

The reverse of this unconscious process of acquiring beliefs is nididhyāsan. It means to consciously create beliefs based upon the divine principles of the scriptures. Through the process of nididhyāsan, we install productive and beneficial convictions in our intellect. By doing so, we unleash a powerful force of self-transformation. When our beliefs are uplifting, then our values are appropriate, attitudes are productive, decisions are proper, and our life progresses in the right direction.

The Vedas go to the extent of saying that if we simply believed in the definition of God, it would uplift our thoughts to great heights and bring our mind to such a state of purity, that we would become God-realised.

astīstyevopalabdhasya tattvabhāvaḥ prasīdati
(*Kaṭhopaniṣhad* 2.3.13)

This mantra from the *Krishna Yajur Veda's Upanishad* section states that though we all intuitively know the definition of God—that He is the creator, all-powerful, all-pervading, and much more—yet we do not really believe it. If only we could believe what we know, we would become God-realised, without doing anything else. What more can be said about the power of beliefs!

An example of this truth was revealed in the life of the great devotee, Prahlad. We all know that God is everywhere, however, the difference was that Prahlad not only knew it, but he also truly believed it as well. His father, the demon King Hiranyakashipu, ordered his servants to kill Prahlad because he worshipped Lord Vishnu. The demons took him away and attempted to put him to death by many means. First, they attacked Prahlad with weapons, but he remained unnerved. Looking at their weapons, Prahlad said:

viṣhṇuḥ śhastreṣhu yuṣhmāsu mayi chāsau vyavasthitaḥ
daiteyāstena satyena mākramantvāyudhāni me
(*Viṣhṇu Purāṇ* 1.17.33)

'My Lord Vishnu is present in these demons and in their weapons; He is also present in me. These weapons can do me no harm.' Subsequently, a fire was lit. Hiranyakashipu's sister, Holika, took Prahlad in her lap, and sat in the fire. She had the boon that fire could not burn her. Sitting in the fire, Prahlad remarked:

tātaiṣha vahniḥ pavaneritopi
na māṁ dahavyatra samantatoham
paśhyāmi padmāstaraṇāstṛitāni
śhītāni sarvāṇi diśhānmukhān.

(*Viṣhṇu Purāṇ* 1.17.47)

'Lord Vishnu is all-pervading; He is in every atom of this fire. I feel as if a sheet of lotus flowers is covering me.' The consequence was that Holika got burned while Prahlad came out intact.

Finally, the demons got the pandits to perform a yajna (fire sacrifice) to create a being who would kill Prahlad. The being that arose from the fire killed the priests instead. Prahlad felt great compassion on seeing the dead pandits. He said:

yathā sarveṣhu bhūteshū sarvavyāpī jagadguruḥ
viṣhṇureva tathā sarve jīvantavene purohitāḥ

(*Viṣhṇu Purāṇ*)

'If my faith is genuine that God is everywhere in this world, may these dead priests come back to life.' The pandits became alive again. The demons took Prahlad to Hiranyakashipu and said, 'We cannot fathom what kind of a boy he is; we have failed to kill him.'

Now, Hiranyakashipu asked Prahlad: *kva sau*? 'Where is this Lord Vishnu whom you worship?' Prahlad answered: *sa sarvatra*. 'Father, He is everywhere.' However, Prahlad pointed in four directions: 'God is in you (a demon); He is in me (a child); He is in this blade of grass (living entity); He is also in this stone pillar (non-living entity).'

Hiranyakashipu sniggered, 'If God is in the stone pillar, then why can I not see Him?' He hit the pillar with all his might. And lo and behold! To prove Prahlad's faith, God manifested from the pillar in the form of Nrisingh Bhagavan. One of the twenty-four descensions of God mentioned in the Shreemad Bhagavatam is Lord Nrisingh, who appeared from the stone pillar of a demon king, proving that God is all-pervading and the whole world is His temple.

This pastime of the Lord and His devotee dramatically illustrates the power of beliefs. Prahlad was just a five-year-old, and yet, the Lord descended for his sake. What made this possible? Prahlad did not just have knowledge of God, he truly had faith in Him—absolute and complete. When that kind of conviction develops, the intellect becomes empowered with tremendous strength. It exerts itself to administer the mind, senses, and body, in alignment with those beliefs.

We have seen how, for good or for bad, faith invests the intellect with immense power. **The process of creating faith, or beliefs, by conscious choice is nididhyāsan. Rather than allowing our intellect to pick up beliefs unconsciously, we consciously choose to establish them based on infallible principles from the scriptures.**

This completes the three-fold process to empower the intellect with divine knowledge. First, we do śhravaṇ (hear or read the knowledge), then manan (contemplate upon it), and then nididhyāsan (develop faith upon it, internalise it, and use it as one's moral compass).

Next, we discuss an even more powerful technique, called *śharaṇāgati,* or surrender to God.

SUMMARY OF THE MAIN POINTS

» To hear or read divine knowledge is shravan. It is the first step in empowering the intellect with wisdom.

» Knowledge, by itself, provides no benefit unless we act upon it. Since we did not implement the divine wisdom of the saints and scriptures, we must hear it again and again, until it gets internalised.

» Knowledge that is forgotten when required is useless. Hence for knowledge to be implemented, it must always remain with us. This requires manan, which means revising the knowledge in our intellect.

» Another Sanskrit word for contemplation is chintan, which refers to the repetition of thoughts. It is a very powerful tool that can be used for our benefit or detriment. Negative chintan devastates while positive chintan elevates.

» Nididhyasan is third and final step in internalising knowledge. It means developing a firm decision of the intellect in alignment with our knowledge.

GETTING THE SUPPORT OF GOD'S GRACE

In previous chapters, we discussed the power of habits, the empowered intellect, contemplation, and much more. These are all very powerful techniques that effectively release our mind from the fetters of vices and beautify us with the ornaments of divine virtues. However, beyond a certain point even these methods cannot help us. They take us to the door of the palace, but they cannot let us in. They need the support of one vital practice that will bring them all to fruition and without which they are as ineffectual as a set of zeros without the one. What is that one practice?

We Cannot Overcome Maya by Our Efforts

While grappling with issues of the mind, we sometimes get so embroiled in the mundane that we often forget there is also a divine perspective. Ultimately, the mind we wish to manage is made of maya. Thus, to conquer the mind means to subjugate maya. Only that person can conquer the mind who can defeat maya.

What is this maya? It is an energy of God working under His supervision. The *Śhwetāśhvatar Upaniṣhad* states:

māyāṁ tu prakṛitiṁ vidyānmāyinaṁ tu maheśhvaram (4.10)

'Maya is the energy (*prakṛiti*), and God is the Energetic to whom it belongs.'

The word 'maya' is derived from the roots *mā* (not) and *yā* (what is). Thus, maya means 'that which is not what it appears to be.' As a shakti of God, maya's service is to veil the true nature of the Supreme Lord from souls who have their face turned away from God. It thus bewilders the souls who are not surrendered to God.

Simultaneously, maya also torments them with the threefold material miseries.[2] In this way, maya tries to help souls realise that they can never be happy until they align themselves with the divine will.

Since maya is animated by His power, it is as powerful as God. Hence, it is unconquerable by self-effort. And since the mind is made from the same material energy, it is equally unrelenting. Even great yogis who perform years of austerities cannot escape its afflictions. Here is a simple story to illustrate this point.

A sadhu practised renunciation in the Himalayas for twelve years. From there, he descended to Haridwar, a holy city on the

[2] According to the Vedic scriptures, there are three root causes for our sorrows: *ādhyātmik* (caused by our thoughts or mind), *ādibhautik* (caused by other living entities), and *ādidaivik* (natural disasters).

banks of the Ganges, to participate in the Kumbh Melā festival and have a sacred dip in the holy river. While walking, his foot accidentally got crushed under someone's shoe, and his nail was shorn off the foot.

Boiling with rage, the sadhu shouted, 'You stupid person! Can you not see? My foot is bleeding!'

Having given vent to his anger, he later realised his folly, 'O what did I do? Twelve years of sadhana in the mountains lost in one moment of indiscretion!'

Such is the power of material energy! Anger, greed, hatred, envy, and illusion, among other negative emotions, are all weapons of maya. Since our mind is material, all these defects exist within each of us. Hence, we cannot succeed in fully uprooting them from inside until the material energy itself releases its hold on us.

Why is material energy keeping us in its grip? Maya is like darkness and God is like light. If we turn away from the light, we will naturally be overcome by darkness. Similarly, we are bound by maya since we have turned our back to God.

What is the means for release from this material energy? The Bhagavad Gita states: *mām eva ye prapadyante māyām etāṁ taranti te* (7.14). Lord Krishna says, 'Arjun, if you surrender to Me, the Supreme Lord, then by My grace, I will take you across the ocean of material existence. I will indicate to maya that this soul has become Mine. Please release him.'

When maya receives God's instruction to release a soul, it says, 'My work was only to keep troubling the soul until it reaches the feet of my Master. Since this soul has now surrendered to God, my work is done.' Understand this through an example from everyday life.

Let us say that you wish to meet your friend. You arrive at his house and casually begin opening the gate. You miss reading the sign on the gate saying 'Beware of dog'.

Your friend's pet German shepherd is standing in the lawn and, as a trained guard dog, growls at you menacingly. Seeing the big, ferocious dog, you decide to go around and try the back gate. However, the German shepherd comes around to the back as well, and snarls furiously, as if to say, 'I dare you to step into this house.'

When you have no other option, you call out to your friend. He emerges from his house and sees his dog troubling you. He calls out, 'No, Smokey! Come and sit here.' The dog is immediately pacified. It goes and sits by its master's side. Now, you open the gate and fearlessly walk in.

In the above example, you were unable to get past the ferocious dog by self-effort. But with the help of its master, you easily coped with the situation. The material energy, maya, is like the dog, and God is its Master. By our own efforts, we can never conquer maya. The only way to overcome it is to take help of its Master who is God.

Our soul (atma), is a tiny fragment of the Supreme Soul, *Paramatma*. In the Bhagavad Gita, Lord Krishna states:

mamaivānśho jīva-loke jīva-bhūtaḥ sanātanaḥ (15.7)

'All the souls of the world are My eternal fragmental parts.' The soul is infinitesimal while God is infinite. You can compare this to a drop of water and the ocean. The drop has the qualities of the ocean—it has identical chemical composition and density. But in terms of quantity or volume, the drop is infinitesimal—a ship can easily sail in the ocean, but not in a drop.

Likewise, God and the soul are both spiritual in quality but different in quantity. God is infinite while the individual soul is finite, and consequently, the effort of the soul is also limited. Hence, **to succeed in managing the mind, the tiny soul needs the support of God's grace.** This one point is so important that it is surprising how it is missed out in personal development workshops and self-help books.

Even the biggest yogis cannot restrain the obdurate mind merely by self-effort. Shri Aurobindo, in his book, *The Mother*, put it very nicely:

> There are two great powers alone that can effect in their conjunction the great and difficult thing that is the aim of our endeavour—a fixed and unfailing aspiration that calls from below and a divine grace that answers from above.

The Vedas state the same thing: *tapaḥ prabhāvād devaprasādāchcha* (*Śhwetāśhvatar Upaniṣhad* 6.21). 'Your efforts and the grace of God, both are essential for success.' Mere self-effort will never suffice. When God bestows His grace on us, we receive His infinite wisdom, strength, power, and purity.

Means to Attract Grace

Divine grace does not descend whimsically upon people. It follows perfectly rational laws. Even a worldly father does not hand over all his precious possessions to his child, until the child becomes responsible enough to utilise them properly. The divine Father is the same. If God did not follow rules while bestowing grace, people's sense of fairness and justice would be shattered.

Let us say, for example, that a father, who is a paddy cultivator, has two sons. During the harvest season, he instructs both of them to work hard in the rice field. One son toils and sweats it out all day long in the blazing sun. At night when he returns, the father says, 'Well done, my son. You are obedient, hard-working, and loyal. Here is your reward. Take Rs 5,000 and do what you like with it.'

The second son does nothing—he lies in bed from morning to night, sleeping, drinking, smoking, and abusing his father. Now suppose the father tells him, 'Never mind, after all, you are also my son. Here is Rs 5,000 for you, too. Go and enjoy yourself.'

On seeing this, the first son's motivation for working hard will be ruined. He will say, 'If this is my father's reward system, then why should I toil so much? I will also do nothing, for I will receive the Rs 5,000 in any case.'

Likewise, if God grants His grace without our becoming qualified, all those who attained sainthood in the past would complain, 'What is this, O Lord? We strived for many lifetimes to purify ourselves and then we became recipients of Your grace, but this person received it without making himself eligible. Then what was the purpose of our efforts for self-improvement?'

Thus, God says, 'I do not behave in an irrational and whimsical manner. I have an eternal law based on which I bestow My grace. And I have declared that law in all the Vedic scriptures.' The *Śhwetāśhvatar Upaniṣhad* states:

yo brahmāṇaṁ vidadhāti pūrvaṁ
yo vai vedānśh cha prahiṇoti tasmai
taṁ ha devam ātma-buddhi-prakāśhaṁ
mumukṣhur vai śharaṇam ahaṁ prapadye (6.18)

'We take shelter of that Supreme Being who created Brahma and others. It is by His grace that the soul and intellect get illumined.' The Shreemad Bhagavatam states:

mām ekam eva śharaṇam ātmānaṁ sarva-dehinām
yāhi sarvātma-bhāvena mayā syā hy akuto-bhayaḥ
(11.12.15)

'O Uddhav! Giving up all forms of mundane social and religious conventions, simply surrender unto Me, the Supreme Soul of all souls. Only then can you cross over this material ocean and become fearless.' The Bhagavad Gita states:

tam eva śharaṇaṁ gachchha sarva-bhāvena bhārata
tat-prasādāt parāṁ śhāntiṁ sthānaṁ prāpsyasi śhāśhvatam
(18.62)

'Surrender exclusively unto Him with your whole being, O scion of Bharat. By His grace, you will attain perfect peace and the eternal abode.' The Ramayan also says:

sanamukha hoi jīva mohi jabahīṅ,
janma koṭi agha nāsahiṅ tabahīṅ

'The moment a soul surrenders to God, its account of sinful deeds from endless past lifetimes is destroyed by His grace.'

Since all the scriptures recommend the act of surrender to the Supreme, let us delve into it more deeply.

The Six Aspects of Surrender

Offering prostrate obeisance to God, chanting His Names, worshipping His deity, meditating upon Him—while all these are beneficial, these cannot, in themselves, be called 'surrender'. One may do all of these and yet not be submitted to the Lord from within. **Śharaṇāgati (surrender) to God is not an external act. It is a state of the consciousness, an internal condition of the mind, intellect, and ego.**

Details of what it means to surrender are explained in a verse that is repeated in many of the Vedic scriptures—*Hari Bhakti Vilās, Bhakti Rasāmṛita Sindhu, Vāyu Purāṇ,* and *Ahir Budhni Sanhitā*:

ānukūlyasya saṅkalpaḥ pratikūlyasya varjanam
rakṣhiṣhyatīti viśhvāso goptṛitve varaṇaṁ tathā
ātmanikṣhepa kārpaṇye ṣhaḍvidhā śharaṇāgatiḥ
(*Hari Bhakti Vilās* 11.676)

This stanza explains the six aspects of surrender to God:

1) To desire only in accordance with the desire of God

By nature, we souls are the servants of God, and the duty of a servant is to fulfil the desire of the master. Therefore, as surrendered devotees of the Lord, we must conform our will to His divine will.

Meerabai, a great bhakti saint of the sixteenth century, expressed this sentiment beautifully when she said: 'If Shree Krishna wishes me to laugh, I will laugh; if He wants me to cry, I will cry; if He desires to shower His love upon me by embracing me, so be it; if He wishes to kill me, using His Sudarśhan Chakra (divine disc that Lord Vishnu holds in His hand), I will not object; and if He chooses to ignore me, as if He does not know me, I will till not complain. No matter what behaviour He adopts towards me, Shree Krishna alone will remain my soul-beloved; in this there will never be any change.'

A dry leaf is surrendered to the wind. It does not complain whether the wind lifts it up, or takes it forward or backward, or drops it to the ground. Similarly, we too must learn to be happy in the happiness of God.

2) Not to desire against the desire of God

This means to not complain about whatever God gives us. Usually, when people get wealth, fame, pleasure, and luxuries of the world, they forget to thank the Creator. However, if they get suffering, they blame Him for it, complaining, 'Why did God do this to me?'

Whatever we get in life is a result of our past and present karmas. But the fruits of the karmas do not accrue by themselves. God notes them and bestows the results at the appropriate time. Since the results are dispensed by the Lord Himself, we must learn to accept them serenely as the following story illustrates.

A boatman was taking fifteen people across a turbulent river. Midway through it, he screamed, 'There is a whirlpool in front and the boat is getting sucked into it, despite my best efforts. God alone can save us now. All of you pray to Him.'

Pandemonium broke loose in the boat. Someone began praying 'Jai Siya Ram', another began chanting 'Jai Mata di', a third person prayed 'Hare Krishna', while yet another recited 'Om Namo Shivaya'.

In the boat, a Babaji (monk) was also sitting. He took out his renunciant's pot and began pouring the river water into the boat. 'What are you doing, Babaji?' everyone asked confused. But Babaji ignored the complaints and continued to fill the boat with water.

After a few minutes, the boatman again announced, 'The whirlpool has moved away; the danger has passed. You all can relax now.' Everyone heaved a sigh of relief.

Babaji now began gathering the water in the boat and throwing it back into the river. People jeered at him, 'Are you crazy, Babaji? First you fill river water into the boat and now you are doing the reverse.'

'Please do not be annoyed,' responded the ascetic. 'I was only trying to surrender to God. When the boatman said that there is no hope, since we were getting sucked into the whirlpool, I concluded that the Lord wants us to die. So I thought let me help Him. That is why I was pouring the river water into the boat. Later, when the boatman declared that the whirlpool has moved away, I thought maybe God has changed His mind, or possibly, I misunderstood His will. He actually wants us all to be saved, so let me help Him

again. That's why I began throwing the water in the boat back into the river.'

This is, of course, a humorous story, but it highlights the concept of surrender very well. A surrendered soul does not desire anything against the will of the Lord.

3) *To have firm faith that God is protecting us*

Typically, a worldly father cares and provides for his children. God is our eternal Father. Why then should we doubt whether He will take care of us or not? He provides for all living beings in creation. There are trillions of ants on Planet Earth and all of them eat regularly. Do you ever find that a few thousand ants in your garden have died of starvation? Nature ensures they are all provided for.

On the other hand, elephants eat mounds of food every day. The universe provides for them too. To have firm faith in the divine protection is the third aspect of surrender. This spirit of faith is highlighted in a story from the Mahabharat.

During the war, Duryodhan taunted Bheeshma, the commander-in-chief of the Kaurav army, saying he was being lenient with the Pandavas, for he could have easily killed them, had he chosen to do so. Bheeshma felt insulted, and resolved that by sunset the next day, he would either kill their foremost warrior, Arjun, or to protect him, Shree Krishna would have to break His vow and lift weapons.

When the battle ended that evening, this news spread in the Pandava camp. Everyone was sad to hear it as Bheeshma was known for keeping his vows. Shree Krishna was lost in contemplation about what could be done. He had vowed not to lift weapons during the war, but now it concerned Arjun's life.

Pondering over the problem, Shree Krishna realised that it was midnight. He thought, 'If I am so concerned, how worried must Arjun be, for it is his death that Grandsire Bheeshma has announced.' He walked over to Arjun's tent to console him. However, He found sounds of snoring emanating from the tent as Arjun was fast asleep.

Shree Krishna shook him awake, 'My dear friend, do you not know about the vow made by Bheeshma?'

'Of course, I do, my Lord.'

'Then are you not worried?'

'When You are so concerned about my protection that You are unable to sleep till early morning, then why should I worry for myself?'

This faith in the protection of God is the third point of surrender. It grows as the *sharaṇāgati* increases.

4) To maintain an attitude of gratitude

We have received so many priceless gifts from the Lord. The earth that we walk upon, the sunlight with which we see, the air we breathe, and the water we drink are all gifts to us by God. In fact, it is because of Him that we exist; He brought us to life and imparted consciousness in our soul. We do not pay Him any tax in return, but at least we ought to feel deeply indebted for all He has given us. This is the sentiment of gratitude.

The reverse is the sentiment of thanklessness. For example, a father does so much for his child. The child is told to be grateful to his father. Instead the child responds, 'His father took care of him and he is taking care of me. Why should I feel gratitude?' This is ungratefulness towards the worldly father. The sentiment of gratitude has a very powerful positive impact upon the mind. In fact, it is the second most positive sentiment after selfless love.

Thus, to be grateful towards our eternal Father, for all that he has given us, is the fourth aspect of surrender.

5) To see all we possess as belonging to the Divine

God created this entire world; it existed before we were born and will continue to exist even after we die. Hence, the true owner of everything is the Supreme Almighty alone. We forget the proprietorship of the Lord when we think something belongs to us.

Let us say that someone comes into your house when you are not at home. He wears your clothes, takes things out of your refrigerator, eats them, and sleeps on your bed. On returning, you ask indignantly, 'What have you been doing in my house?'

He says, 'I have not damaged anything. I have merely put it to good use. Why are you getting annoyed?'

You reply, 'You may not have destroyed anything, but it all belongs to me. If you use it without my permission, you are a thief.'

Similarly, this world and everything in it is the property of God. To remember this and renounce our sense of proprietorship is the fifth aspect of surrender.

6) To relinquish the pride of having surrendered

If we become proud of our good deeds, the pride soils our heart and undoes the good we have done. That is why it is important to keep an attitude of humility and think in the following manner: 'If I was able to do something worthwhile, it was only because God inspired my intellect in the right direction. Left to myself, I would never have succeeded.'

Consider the following example.

Once a sadhu (ascetic) practised austerities in the Himalayas, while sitting on a single boulder. After twelve years, he had a divine experience. His heart was thrilled with divine bliss and he heard the voice of God. 'Sadhu! I am pleased with your dedication,' God said. 'You have strived sincerely. Now ask for a boon.'

'Of course, I will ask for a boon. I have worked so hard; why should I not ask?' the sadhu replied.

God was quiet. He had not expected such an immodest reply. After a few minutes, He again spoke from the sky, 'Sadhu, are you asking for My causeless grace or are you asking for the fruit of your hard work?'

The sadhu retorted, 'Who is begging for Your grace, my Lord? I am interested in the fruit of my effort; please bestow it upon me.'

God was quiet again. Then after a while, the boulder upon which the sadhu was sitting began speaking, 'O Lord, since this sadhu is demanding to settle his accounts with You, please also settle my accounts with him. He has been sitting on me for the last twelve years. For the next twelve years, please make me sit upon him.'

The sadhu quickly realised his folly.

We can never settle accounts with God. Whenever He bestows His grace, it is always causeless, and we should never be proud, claiming that we deserved it. Thus, to keep an attitude of humility is the sixth aspect of surrender.

If we can perfect these six attitudes within ourselves, we will fulfil God's condition for śharaṇāgati and become recipients of His grace.

Using All Techniques in the Spirit of Surrender

Had we been fully aligned with the divine will, we would have received God's grace and become perfect. There would be no need for other practices of mind management. However, since we are still a far cry away from complete surrender, we must practise the other techniques as well. Together, they all will help us reach the state of complete śharaṇāgati.

The trick then is to practice the tools of mind management externally, while internally depending upon God's grace. That was the advice given by Maharshi Vasishth to Lord Ram: *kartā bahir akartāntaraloke vihara rāghava* (*Yog Vāsiṣhṭh*). 'Ram, externally put your best efforts into the sadhana. Internally, pray for God's grace for success.'

In this way, śharaṇāgati and other techniques in this book must be practised together. The tools of mind management will help us perfect our surrender, and the process of surrender will augment these techniques. They complement each other.

A question that may come to the mind at this stage is whether it is possible to maintain a normal family life and still submit to God? How does śharaṇāgati affect our worldly life? This brings us to the principle of karm yog (yoga of action), which we will review in the next chapter.

SUMMARY OF THE MAIN POINTS

» The mind is made from maya, and hence, it can only be controlled by one who can overcome maya.

» Maya is God's energy and it has His power behind it. It is unconquerable by even the biggest yogis and ascetics.

» Conquest of the mind requires the grace of God. Sheer willpower does not suffice.

» God bestows His grace when we surrender to Him. This is His eternal law which He has stated in all the religious traditions of the world.

» Surrender requires the fulfilment of six conditions :

1. To desire only in accordance with the desire of God
2. Not to desire against the desire of God
3. To have firm faith that God is protecting us
4. To maintain an attitude of gratitutde towards God
5. To see all we possess as belonging to God
6. To relinquish the pride of having surrendered

» If we were fully surrendered, we would have no need for other practices. But since we are yet far from being surrendered, we should practice other techniques as well. They will help us reach the state of complete surrender.

KARM YOG FOR EVERYDAY LIVING

In the previous chapter, we discussed śharaṇāgati as the means for conquering material energy, maya, and its child, the mind. Surrender seems to be a wonderful idea for attaining the Supreme, but does it really have any relevance to our everyday existence?

Human life is multi-faceted, and while living in the world, we must wear many hats. We have family, professional, social, religious duties, and so on. In the process of balancing all these, we experience a plethora of problems, such as stress, anxiety, and fear, among others. How can we manage our mind in the midst of all these tribulations?

This is where the science of karm yog proves invaluable, for it gives people in household life clear guidance on how to perform their duties with a calm and serene mind, free from anxiety and stress.

Stress – the Anathema of Modern Life

John Rockefeller, the richest person in the world in his time, had a business decision to make. The Standard Oil Corporation required *the transportation of goods by train, from Houston to Chicago. The insurance of the cargo would have cost $150. Rockefeller was in a dilemma whether to have the goods insured or not. He decided to take a risk and save the insurance expense. As luck would have it, a snowstorm developed on the way. When he came to know of it, Rockefeller was besieged by anxiety. He lamented his choice and decided to use his clout to coerce the insurance company into giving him last-minute insurance coverage. It was late evening; the company had closed its office for the day. Rockefeller contacted the manager at his home and forced him to open the office. By ten o'clock at night he was able to procure the insurance.*

Next morning, he received the news that the train had safely reached Chicago, and there was no damage to the goods. Rockefeller was so upset at having spent $150 unnecessarily that he could not get to work until two o'clock in the afternoon.

The stress of business took a heavy toll on Rockefeller's health. Doctors warned him that his physical condition was critical, and that if he continued in the same manner, he would not survive. That shook him up. He changed his priorities and developed an interest in other pursuits, besides earning money. He set up the Rockefeller Foundation that did remarkable philanthropic work around the world. His change in attitude towards work had a salubrious effect on his health and he lived for another twenty-five years.

This account is from the nineteenth century. Today, in the twenty-first century, stress has become a widespread ailment. While we march forward boldly in harnessing material nature with ever-new technologies, when it comes to the conquest of the mind, humankind seems to be standing still. As the world speeds up with Instagram, WhatsApp, Twitter, Facebook, and smartphones, an increasing number of people complain of stress. It is particularly common among high-achieving company executives and is sometimes called the 'executive's disease'. Stress creates a gamut of negative emotions like tension, fear, distress, apprehension, and anxiety. On the physical level, it causes health problems such as headaches, acidity, ulcers, high blood pressure, obesity, and heart disease.

How do we define stress? For an engineer, stress is the force in a beam or a machine part that tends to distort, crush, bend, or break it. We humans too are subjected to forces at home, at work, and in the world at large. The tension **and anxiety in our emotional being, as we adjust to our continually changing environment, is what we call 'stress'.** The situations for stress can be innumerable. As babies, we experienced stress when we were hungry and cried out to our mother. As grown-ups, we experience it when our boss hints that our performance is unsatisfactory, and we will soon lose our job. As parents, we feel it when our children do not get good grades at school or are not admitted to the school of our choice.

Before we get into the techniques of stress management, understand the distinction between the emotional stress within us and the stressful situations outside. Stressful situations are not harmful in themselves; they are catalysts for progress. They inspire us to develop our abilities, as we attempt to face them. A world without stressful situations would be as insipid as a class without exams. Good teachers never permit the latter and God never sanctions the former. The Creator has designed the world in such a way that it continually throws up challenges and obstacles in our path. Swami Vivekananda said: 'Life is the continuous unfoldment of a being under circumstances tending to press it downwards.'

Hence, our goal is not to eliminate stressful situations. Instead, we wish to eliminate the emotional stress generated within us while responding to these situations. This stress varies from person to person. Someone may be perfectly calm and adjusted while administering a country; another person may be a nervous wreck while managing a single family. Thus, the stress we experience is dependent on our own inner psyche and not on external situations.

Why Stress Develops

How can we reduce or eliminate stress? Stress management consultants offer a plethora of solutions for reducing stress. They talk about time management, situation management, meditation, yoga, tai chi, and a host of other techniques to combat stress. However, these techniques are ineffective as they deal with the symptoms of stress without addressing the source. It is like suppressing fever without curing the typhoid that caused it. If we wish to be free of stress, we must get rid of its root cause—the flawed mental thinking that leads to it. Thus, the first step in stress management is to try to understand the origin of stress.

Stress develops when we are attached to a particular outcome and worried that things may not turn out as we desire. If a businessperson wants to make profits, but runs into losses, he experiences stress. If a sales representative wishes to meet a particular sales target, but fails to do so, stress ensues. Thus, it is clear that stress is caused by our own attachment to a particular outcome and our unwillingness to accept other possible results.

Once we understand the cause, the remedy for stress is simple—give up attachment to preconceived or wishful outcomes of our efforts. **Put in your best efforts without attachment to the results.** The Bhagavad Gita instructs: *karmaṇy-evādhikāras te mā phaleṣhu kadāchana* (2.47). 'You have a right to perform your work, but you are not entitled to the fruits of your actions.' Relish your work and offer the fruit of your efforts to God.

The outcome of our efforts is, in any case, not in our hands. It depends upon several factors, such as circumstances, assistance from others, efforts of competitors, sheer luck, coincidence, God's will, and other factors not always within our control. Thus, wisdom demands that we put in our best efforts and be content with whatever results we get.

Examples of Work Without Attachment

Though it may seem alien in common everyday life, the philosophy of working without attachment to results is not a new kind of activity that we have never heard of. Consider the following example of a nurse.

A nurse in a hospital tends to patients with great care and attention. If the patient dies, the nurse does not lament; if the patient recuperates, she does not celebrate. She merely performs her duty. But if one of the patients happens to be related to her, she experiences intense anxiety while performing her duty. In this case, she is attached, while with the rest of the patients, she was only doing her duty.

Likewise, there are innumerable examples of working without attachment.

A cashier in a bank receives and disburses millions of rupees. In doing so, he experiences neither anxiety nor jubilation although he works with great care and diligence. But if he withdraws his own salary and accidentally drops a 2,000 rupee note from it on the way home, he is terribly upset when he discovers his mistake. He is attached to his money, while at the bank, he simply does his duty.

The above illustrations highlight how we perform a number of tasks in the world without attachment. Now, if we can learn to do this at all times and in all situations, we will have a permanent solution to stress and discover blissful peace. The Bhagavad Gita states.

vihāya kāmān yaḥ sarvān pumānśh charati niḥspṛihaḥ
nirmamo nirahankāraḥ sa śhāntim adhigachchhati (2.71)

'That person who gives up all material desires and lives free from a sense of greed, proprietorship, and egoism, attains perfect peace.'

I refer to such an attitude with the acronym NATO not implying the well-known 'North Atlantic Treaty Organization', but rather 'Not Attached to Outcome'. Let us see how effective NATO is by first applying it to a simple activity like a game of golf.

When people play golf, they always concentrate on the outcome of the game, which is their score on the board. They get so worked up about how much under- or over-par their score is that they miss out on enjoying the shots they play. For them, the game is all about the score which is the outcome of their efforts. The score then becomes the primary source of happiness, and enjoyment of the game itself is secondary. If the score is good, they become happy, and if it is bad, they become sad. Instead, if they stop thinking of the score for a while, and just play their shots with focus and relish, they will find great joy in every shot they play. They will also play the best golf of their life, because they will not be distracted by anxieties of the past or concerns about the future. In this manner, they will be totally absorbed in the present moment.

Similarly, the concept of NATO is applicable to more complex activities such as work in professional organisations. Just focus on your efforts without anxiety about the outcome.

This statement gives rise to a question: 'If we give up attachment to results, will it not decrease our performance and effectiveness at work?'

The question is natural, and, no, our performance will definitely not decrease. In fact, when we become free from negative emotions like tension, anxiety, apprehension, and nervousness, our effectiveness will only increase. For example, businesspeople and athletes know that if they become anxious or nervous during interviews, negotiations, or in the middle of a match, they are liable to commit mistakes. This is one reason people keep telling you to 'keep your cool' as it is an implied reference to detachment from the outcome.

Similarly, competent surgeons perform hundreds of surgeries on others, but they are never willing to operate on their own child. They know that attachment makes them prone to error.

Dr Mukherjee is a fifty-five-year-old surgeon. He has conducted over 5,000 surgeries in his life. But today, Dr Mukherjee's wife is unwell. Will he perform a surgery on her? The chances are that he will say, 'I'm too attached. I'll make some mistakes. I'll call my friend. I can't do it.' He is too nervous to conduct a surgery on his wife. Why? Because his attachment to the result—his wife's well-being—will undermine his confidence and competence.

Thus, detachment from results always helps us perform better. With the mind focused totally on the efforts, we work with more calm, balance, and poise. Recent research and investigations in the West support this principle.

Modern Writers' Perspective

The modern generation's focus on setting goals and achieving them has generated countless books in the last several decades. There are even books on goal-setting for children! In this context, goals equate to results. Achieving specific measurable results is how success is measured in the corporate environment. At one time, Management By Results (MBR), took the business world by storm. While titles and verbiage have changed over the years, the desired end result is the same: goals, objectives, results, bottom line, achievements.

The MBR approach is definitely useful in helping people with systematic planning. It helps achieve clarity of thought and focus upon the goals. But the big danger in the 'results-are-everything' approach is that people become conditioned to believing that happiness lies only in the destination. They miss out on the joy of the effort. Consequently, some contemporary thinkers have begun questioning this 'happiness is only in the result' attitude.

Thomas C. Corley, author of the popular *Rich Habits – The Daily Success Habits of Wealthy Individuals*, studied and interviewed two hundred millionaires over five years of research. He writes in his blog that he was very surprised to learn that they worked hard every day, not hoping for a specific big reward, but because they liked what they were doing and believed that hard work would pay off one day. 'Just put in your best everyday' was their consistent message. Some even said they did not have expectations for a definite outcome! Their most important realisation was that they could only control their efforts not the outcomes. As a result, they were not wasting mental energy on expectations and worries about achieving specific goals. Their mental resources were free for focusing on their work and putting in their best effort.

Another author, Joshua Becker, named as a best-selling author by *The Wall Street Journal* for his book, *Simplify: 7 Guiding Principles to Help Anyone Declutter Their Home & Life*, writes in his blog, *Not Just The Outcome, But The Process* that experiencing happiness only upon achieving an outcome for our efforts 'robs us of countless moments along the way'. Focusing on results alone leads to a good deal of our life being experienced as drudgery, something to be endured until we achieve the summit, our goal. For example, we admire a well-kept lawn and flower garden, but have been conditioned to see the necessary steps to achieve it as tedious labour. Our appreciation of the lawn would have been deeper, if we had also considered the labour that had gone into making it beautiful as joyful instead of tedious.

If we simply focus on the present moment, on the joy of our labour, we will unleash our intelligence and experience creativity in our work. We will then give our best efforts and let the results follow.

Becker concludes that the results-only focus is short-sighted and distracts us from applying ourselves to what we can control, which is our time and energy. It discounts the role of work and effort in our lives. It neglects the value of exercising discipline in our daily schedule. And furthermore, it robs us of the feeling of satisfaction in the steps along the way. When we believe that happiness can only be experienced in the future, on reaching the goal, we miss out on enjoying the journey towards it, which is in the present.

Next, a compelling case is made by Tom Murcko in his blog, *Focus on Process, Not Outcome* for putting our attention on actions and not on uncertain results. He says: 'It seems like the best way to reach a desired result would be to focus on that result, try to move toward it, and judge each attempt by how closely you approximate it. But actually that approach is far from optimal. If you focus your attention less on the results you're hoping for, and more on the processes you use, you will learn faster and be happier with the outcome.'

Tom Murcko explains that focusing on the process rather than the outcome is a far better strategy. It has the following advantages:

- it encourages experimentation, allows more opportunity for serendipity, and creates more possibilities for stumbling on an even better outcome than what we were initially aiming for.
- It lets us enjoy the process and allows us to engage more deeply with the present.
- It puts us in control. Putting in our best effort is completely within our control.

- It does not make our happiness contingent on a specific outcome. Happiness comes from knowing that we put in our hundred per cent.

We see how modern thinkers are also reaching the conclusion that getting stressed about outcomes is counterproductive. Instead, focusing on efforts is a better style of working and one that eliminates stress.

This conclusion reiterates the perennial knowledge of the Bhagavad Gita:

kāyena manasā buddhyā kevalair indriyair api
yoginah karma kurvanti saṅgaṁ tyaktvātma-śhuddhaye
(5.11)

'The yogis, while giving up attachment, perform actions with their body, senses, mind, and intellect, only for the purpose of self-purification.' Let us now see how we can incorporate this into a comprehensive philosophy of life through the principle of karm yog.

Karm Yog – The Art of Working in Divine Consciousness

If attachment is the root cause of stress, how can we get rid of it? The Bhagavad Gita gives a simple answer. It tells us not to give up attachment, rather transfer it to the Supreme Divine Personality. This is the principle of karm yog. A karm yogi is one who keeps the mind equipoised, while engaged in the tumult of worldly works.

How is that done? Karm yog is the synthesis of both 'karm' (occupational duties) and 'yog' (union with God). 'Body in the world and mind in God.' A karm yogi performs worldly duties with the body while the mind is attached to God.

There have been many karm yogis in Indian history, such as Dhruv, Prahlad, Ambarish, Prithu, and Yudhishthir, to name a few. All of them were great emperors who were constantly surrounded by people and had to fulfil many complex tasks for the administration of their kingdom, and yet, internally their consciousness was always absorbed in the Lord.

The practice of karm yog is the main focus of the Bhagavad Gita. It teaches us not to artificially renounce work, thinking of it as cumbersome; instead, to be in internal equilibrium even while doing complex tasks.

The listener of the Bhagavad Gita, Arjun, said, 'I wish to abdicate my professional duty. It is too disturbing and confusing.'

Lord Krishna replied, 'No, Arjun! You have your responsibility to family, society, and the path of righteousness. Do not give it up, rather be a karm yogi.'

sarveṣhu kāleṣhu mām anusmara yudhya cha

(Bhagavad Gita 8.7)

'Remember Me at all times and continue to work.'

Jagadguru Kripalu-ji Maharaj also emphasised karm yog in his teachings:

mana hari meṅ tana jagata meṅ, karm yog yehi jāna
tana hari meṅ mana jagata meṅ, yaha mahāna ajñāna

(*Bhakti Śhatak* verse 84)

'If the body is engaged in the world and the mind is in God, that is karm yog. The reverse of this is gross ignorance—where the body is engaged in God and the mind is in the world.'

Saint Kabir taught the same principle in simple language:

sumirana kī sudhi yauṅ karo, jyoṅ surabhi suta māhiñ
kahe kabīra charo charata bisarata kabahunka nāhiñ

'Remember God as a cow remembers its calf. It grazes grass in the field all day but keeps its mind in the calf.'

When the mind is in the Supreme, we naturally work for His pleasure, offering the results of our efforts to Him. Again, the Bhagavad Gita states:

yat karoṣhi yad aśhnāsi yaj juhoṣhi dadāsi yat
yat tapasyasi kaunteya tat kuruṣhva mad-arpaṇam (9.27)

'Whatever you do, whatever you eat, whatever sacrifices you perform, whatever you give away in charity, and whatever austerities you undertake, do them all as an offering unto Me.'

Benefits of the Practice of Karm Yog

Keeping the mind in yog and yoked to the divine while going about our daily tasks is very powerful. Since the mind is in the divine realm, our perspective becomes divine towards everything—people, work, ourselves, results, and failure. The technique of karm yog bestows many benefits:

First, we see ourselves as fragments of the divine. Such an attitude allows us to develop a healthy self-identity, not based on ego or who people think we are, but on the reality of our soul. We maintain humility without being self-demeaning.

Second, we see our work as service to the divine. The work becomes, not drudgery to go through, but a joy to perform. As a result, we exert ourselves with a positive attitude, to the best of our ability, for the pleasure of God.

Third, since the results of our efforts are for the pleasure of the Supreme, we are not attached to them. If we do not get the desired results despite our best exertions, we think, 'Probably, it was not the will of the Lord. Let me submit to His wish and be happy.' This sense of detachment frees us from stress, anxiety, tension, and fear.

Fourth, we view everyone with whom we interact as divine fragments of God and consequently we maintain a healthy attitude towards them. Our interpersonal interactions are positive and service-oriented.

Fifth, when we keep God in our consciousness, we realise that His grace makes all things possible, and, in turn, are freed from the pride of doership.

Sixth, the goal of human life is God-realisation. In karm yog, we move towards this goal together with doing our worldly duties.

We have seen the efficacy and benefits of karm yog. **In this way, karm yogis live in the world but do not let the world live in them.** However, it is important to draw attention to the most vital aspect of this practice which is to always keep the consciousness linked to God.

Constant Remembrance of God

Often people claim they are karm yogis. When asked to explain, they say, 'I do yog for half hour every morning, and then, I focus on karm throughout the day. Since I do both "karm" and "yog", I am also a karm yogi.' However, this is an incorrect interpretation.

Karm yog is constant absorption of the mind in God, along with doing our worldly-duties.

As long as our mind is in the divine realm, it is away from the material sentiments of anger, hatred, resentment, fear, greed, and anxiety. And when remembrance of God becomes continuous, the state of divine union through work is achieved.

Therefore, the condition for karm yog—always keep your mind in God—is repeatedly emphasised in many verses of the Bhagavad Gita:

sarveṣhu kāleṣhu mām anusmara yudhya cha (8.7)

'At all times, remember Me and do your duty.'

ananya-chetāḥ satataṁ yo māṁ smarati nityaśhaḥ (8.14)

'Keep your mind absorbed in Me through exclusive devotion. Always think of Me.'

satataṁ kīrtayanto māṁ yatantaśh cha dṛiḍha-vratāḥ (9.14)

'Always glorify Me and strive with great determination.'

teṣhāṁ nityābhiyuktānāṁ yoga-kṣhemaṁ vahāmyaham (9.22)

'If your mind is always absorbed in Me, I will protect you in all ways.' All these verses inform us that we must keep our mind uninterruptedly fixed in the Supreme as we go about our daily duties.

On hearing the principle of karm yog, people often ask, 'If we continuously think of the Lord, how will we be able to do our regular work?' The question is natural because no work can be done without the application of the mind.

The answer is, in fact, quite simple. **Karm yog does not require that we focus upon God, but rather, that we attach the mind to Him.** This does not require us to learn something new. We already know how to work with attachment elsewhere. Consider the three examples below:

1) *One person works eight-to-five in the office with the mind attached to golf. He keeps thinking, 'When will it be six o'clock in the evening and I'll get out of the office and to the golf course?'*
2) *Another person is attached to alcohol. He thinks, 'When will my work get over and I will sip a margarita with my friends?'*
3) *Yet another person is the CEO of a Fortune 500 company. People say she is most proficient in her work. But the fact is that she has no attachment to the organisation and is only working for the money she gets. If a competing organisation were to offer one-and-a-half times the salary, she will willingly say goodbye to the current employer. Her attachment is not to work, but to her family, status, and possessions. The work is only a means of fulfilling these.*

These are examples of working in one place with attachment elsewhere. We all know how to work in this manner. A small modification in this can make us karm yogis. **The principle of karm yog says: Keep your mind attached to the Lord alone—nowhere else in the world—and continue doing your work.**

This leads us to the next question: How can we achieve the state of constant attachment in God? A powerful technique is described in the following section.

Practice of the Presence of God

How can we perceive the presence of God all the time? Throughout our waking state, we constantly perceive ourselves: 'I am eating', 'I am walking', 'I am thinking', 'I am speaking', and so on. However, we fail to remember the presence of God who always resides within our hearts. We are conscious of 'I am' but forget to realise 'God is also with me'.

We must now add this perception to our consciousness: 'I am not alone. God is always accompanying me. He is my Witness and my Protector.' In fact, God is everywhere and all-pervading, but we have forgotten to realise His presence. Now we need to make space for Him in our consciousness and practice realising His constant presence with us.

Most of us do acknowledge the presence of God when we visit a place of worship such as a temple, church, mosque, gurdwara, or synagogue. However, we forget Him as soon as we walk out. This partial concept—that God is present only in the temple—affects our attitude. It makes us hypocrites with double standards—be ethical and devotional in the temple, but when outside, do as you wish.

Because we limit our perception of God to just the temple, we lower our standard for ethical behaviour. Instead, if we reminisced that the whole world is His temple and He is watching us everywhere, we would never indulge in sin anywhere. We would keep up a high standard of ethics and morality at all times.

A Christian monk, Brother Lawrence of the Resurrection, who served as a lay brother in a Carmelite monastery in Paris, also described the same technique in his diary. He wrote: 'If I were a preacher, I would preach nothing but the practice of the presence of God.' His writings were discovered after his death and later published as a book, *The Practice of the Presence of God.*

How can we implement this technique in our daily routine? Let us say, you go to your office and sit on your chair in the morning. Take a pause before you start work. First, make God sit on an empty chair in one corner of the room. Think, 'Shree Krishna is watching me. All I am doing is for His pleasure and in His service'. Now, begin your work.

Since, we are not yet accomplished karm yogis, it is natural that as we get engrossed in our work, God will slip out of our mind. Never mind. After an hour, stop work, and again think, 'God is watching me. He is saying, "Aay ... you were supposed to keep your mind in Me. What have you started thinking?"' In this way, our consciousness that had slipped down will again get uplifted. The stream of poor thoughts that had begun flowing in our mind will stop.

We must keep practising in this manner after every hour. Once we have established the practice at intervals of one hour, then increase the frequency to every half hour. When that is achieved, increase the frequency further to intervals of fifteen minutes. With constant practice, the stage will be reached where we will continuously feel the presence of God with us.

Practice Leads to Perfection

The technique of karm yog has been described in detail in the previous section. But bear in mind that the state of constant remembrance of God will not be achieved without effort. It requires a lot of practice just as all the other skills we learn in the world.

When we were children and sat on a bicycle for the first time, we found it difficult to multi-task—peddle with the feet, hold the handle, keep the balance, and look at the road ahead. We would fall despite our focused efforts. After sufficient practice, riding a bicycle became natural. Now, when we ride it, the feet keep peddling on their own, and we can even speak to others at the same time. This dexterity came through practice. Similarly, the exercise of karm yog will become natural with repeated effort.

The beauty of the technique 'practice of the presence of God' is that it is inconspicuous. It can naturally be added to our daily life without the need for rosary beads or any kind of ostentation. Instead, if we choose chanting beads to remember God, and take them to office, it will invoke the cynicism of others, requiring explanations and clarifications. The attention we invite will distract us from divine remembrance. For this reason, the scriptures advise us to hide our spiritual practice from public view:

gopanīyaṁ gopanīyaṁ gopanīyaṁ prayatnataḥ

'Keep your sadhana private.' **Conceal your sadhana from the world to avoid becoming a victim of pride and hypocrisy.** The practice of the presence of God is a beautiful way of remembering Him without having people raise eyebrows.

Success in karm yog requires cleaning our consciousness and absorbing it in the divine. Therefore, let us next discuss a technique for deep cleansing of the mind and loving absorption in God. This is the wonderful technique of affirmation or positive self-talk.

SUMMARY OF THE MAIN POINTS

» The tension and anxiety in our emotional being as we adjust to our continually changing environment is what we call 'stress'.

» Stressful situations are not harmful in themselves; they are catalysts for progress.

» Stress gets eliminated when we become detached from the results of our actions and simply focus on the effort.

» When we are Not Attached To Outcome (NATO), we are able to do our work even better and in a more joyous state of mind.

» A karm yogi is one who performs worldly duties with the body while the mind is united with God 'Body in the world and mind in God.'

- The practice of Karm yog demands the constant remembrance of God while doing any and all work. This is accomplished by attaching the mind to Him.
- A wonderful technique for the implementation of karm yog is the practice of the presence God. Keep realising His presence at frequent intervals of time. Slowly, the experience of His presence with us will become continuous.

POSITIVE SELF-TALK AND AFFIRMATION

We have seen how we are what our mind is for our consciousness is tied to it. Therefore, we need to purify not just the top layers of the mind but even its innermost depths. When we get down to cleaning it, we will realise that it is far deeper than we had imagined. Just as the ocean is immensely deep below, with tiny waves on the surface, the mind too has its conscious and subconscious aspects.

We are aware of the conscious mind, for we observe its negativity, fluctuations, and mood-shifts. But we do not understand that ninety per cent of these perturbations are inspired by the subconscious mind of which we are not even aware.

The Subconscious Origin of Our Attitudes

The subconscious mind is a huge memory bank carrying images, experiences, grudges, phobias, and endless other events and emotions from the past. It is like a bottomless well; there are no limits as to how much it can store. These subliminal memories from the past influence our conscious thoughts and attitudes. For example:

A four-year-old girl got stuck in an elevator. She was alone and had no one to turn to. She felt extreme fear, isolation, and uncertainty until she came out of it. The distressing incident was experienced by the conscious mind. As the months went by, the girl forgot about the event. Nevertheless, its memories remained in the subconscious and continued with her into adulthood. Even now, when she enters a car, she feels claustrophobic. She cannot figure out why she has this irrational fear of closed spaces, and hence, cannot overcome it.

Consider another example.

A boy was terribly threatened by a ferocious dog in infancy. In a few months, the incident was forgotten by his conscious memory. But the incident remained embedded in the subconscious mind and he continues to experience a phobia for dogs even in adulthood. The conscious mind is disturbed by the inexplicable fear. The intellect repeatedly tries to coach the mind that such a phobia is dysfunctional and baseless, and yet he is unable to break its grip over the mind. This is a case where images and fears embedded deep in the subconscious hold sway over the conscious mind.

This mechanism does not apply only to phobias. It is also true for many of our other attitudes, likes, and dislikes. The subconscious mind is like a child—it holds memories and creates sentiments, but it cannot logically reason whether they are beneficial or harmful. The conscious mind is aware of these feelings and sentiments affecting it from deep inside but is often unaware of the source from where these arise.

Sigmund Freud referred to the subconscious mind as the 'unconscious mind'. He went to the extent of hypothesising that the unconscious mind has a will and purpose of its own, which cannot be known to the conscious mind, and hence, termed it 'unconscious'. He considered it a repository for socially unacceptable ideas, desires, traumatic memories, and painful emotions thrown out of conscious awareness by the mechanism of psychological repression.

Modern psychiatry sanctions the use of hypnotherapy to regress patients to earlier stages in their life under the spell of hypnosis. Such guided regression of patients with the help of certified hypnotherapists enables patients to discover the source of the troublesome behaviour in their past experiences. Once the awareness comes in the conscious mind, they are able to stop the distressing behaviour with remarkable ease.

However, Sigmund Freud would have been astonished to hear that our subconscious mind is not of just one lifetime; it continues with the soul since innumerable past lifetimes!

The Concept of Rebirth

The Bhagavad Gita explains the phenomenon of rebirth:

dehino 'smin yathā dehe kaumāraṁ yauvanaṁ jarā
tathā dehāntara-prāptir dhīras tatra na muhyati (2.13)

'Just as the embodied soul continuously passes from childhood to youth to old age, similarly, at the time of death, the soul passes into another body. The wise are not deluded by this.'

In this verse, using immaculate logic, Lord Krishna establishes the principle of transmigration of the soul from lifetime to lifetime. He explains that in one lifetime itself, we change bodies from childhood to youth to maturity and then to old age.

In fact, modern science informs us that cells within the body undergo regeneration—old cells die and new ones take their place. It is estimated that practically all the cells in the body change every seven years. And yet, despite the continual change of the body, we perceive that we are the same person. That is because we are not the material body, but the spiritual soul seated within.

Since the physical body is constantly changing, the soul passes through many bodies in one lifetime itself. Similarly, at the time of death, it passes into another body. Actually, what we term as 'death' in worldly parlance is merely the soul discarding its old dysfunctional body, and what we call 'birth' is the soul taking on a new body elsewhere.

The *Nyāya Darśhan* presents the following argument to prove the existence of rebirth:

stanyābhilāṣhāt (3.1.21)

It says that a new-born baby has no knowledge of language. How then can a mother teach her baby to suckle when she inserts her breast into the baby's mouth? Since the new-born child has drunk milk in infinite past lifetimes—even in animal forms, from the breasts, teats, and udders of innumerable mothers—based on past practice, when the mother puts her breast in the baby's mouth, it automatically begins suckling.

The *Nyāya Darśhan* gives another argument in support of rebirth:

jātasya harṣhabhayaśhoka sampratipatteḥ (3.1.18)

If you observe a little baby, you will find it is sometimes happy, sad, or fearful, without any apparent reason. According to the *Nyāya Darśhan*, the little baby is remembering its past life, and hence, experiencing these emotions. However, as it grows up, the impressions of the present life fall so strongly upon the mind that they erase most past memories. Even prior to that, the processes of death and birth are so painful to the soul that they erase a substantial portion of past life memories.

The passage of the soul upon death from one body to another is called the principle of reincarnation. Most Oriental philosophies accept this concept of reincarnation. It is an integral part of Hinduism, Jainism, and Sikhism. In Buddhism, the Buddha referred to His past lives repeatedly.

Many people are not aware of the extent to which reincarnation was a part of the belief system of the Occidental philosophies as well. In ancient classical Western religious and philosophic circles, famous thinkers such as Pythagoras, Plato, and Socrates accepted reincarnation to be true, and their views were also reflected in Orphism, Hermeticism, Neoplatonism, Manicheanism, and Gnosticism.

Without accepting the concept of rebirth, it is difficult to make sense out of the suffering, chaos, and incompleteness of the world, and hence, many famous Western thinkers believed in this principle. If, instead of accepting the phenomenon of rebirth, we believe that this life is our first entry into existence and there is no life after death, then the disparity between human beings becomes inexplicable and irrational.

For example, let us suppose a man is blind from birth and he asks why he was punished in this way, what answer can be given to him? If we say it was a result of his karmas (actions), he may argue that the present life is the only life he has, and therefore, there are no past karmas at the time of birth that should afflict him. If we say it was the will of God, it would also seem implausible, since God is all-merciful and would not unnecessarily want anyone to be blind. The only logical explanation is that the person was born blind as a consequence of karmas from past lives. Thus, from common sense and on the authority of the scriptures, we are obliged to believe in the concept of rebirth.

In recent times, Dr Brian Weiss has done tremendous work in popularising the concept of reincarnation in the Western world. His book, *Many Lives Many Masters*, was a bestseller for many years and his workshops on past-life regression are attended by millions of people.

Transmigration of the Soul

If the soul is continuing from previous births, then how does its transmigration take place? The Bhagavad Gita explains:

> *vāsānsi jīrṇāni yathā vihāya, navāni gṛihṇāti naro 'parāṇi*
> *tathā śharīrāṇi vihāya jīrṇānya, nyāni sanyāti navāni dehī*
> (2.22)

'As a person sheds worn-out garments and wears new ones, likewise, at the time of death, the soul casts off its worn-out body and enters a new one.'

The Vedic scriptures further explain that each individual soul is bound by three bodies—gross, subtle, and causal body.

1) Gross body: consists of the five gross elements of nature—earth, water, fire, air, and space.
2) Subtle body: consists of mind, intellect, and ego (to explain it simply).
3) Causal body: consists of the account of karmas from endless past lives, including sanskārs (tendencies) from previous lives.

At the time of death, the soul discards only its gross body, while the subtle and causal bodies continue with it. In the next life, the soul receives another gross body corresponding to its subtle and causal bodies. **Thus, the subtle and causal bodies continue with the soul from past lifetimes.** This explains why someone who is blind from birth also sees dreams.

What is the dream state? While dreaming, the intellect is asleep, but the mind is still active. During this state, since the mind is not governed by the intellect, it throws up garbled and jumbled impressions.

Consider for example that in the waking state, you saw a bird, and thought, 'How wonderful would it be if I were a bird and could fly in the air!' In the dream state, you did not become a bird but began flying in the human body itself. Now you may wonder why you dreamed of flying? The reason was that your thoughts and resolves in the waking state became garbled and reconfigured.

In this way, dreams are a rehash of what we see in the waking state. However, the astonishing thing is that people who are blind from birth also see dreams. The reason is that images are embedded in the subconscious from past lives.

This also explains the phenomenon of déjà vu, where we see something, and the mind has the nagging feeling that we have seen it before, but we cannot figure out where.

We thus conclude that our subconscious is not of one life but of innumerable lifetimes. Though the gross body changes in every life, the subtle and the causal bodies continue with the soul upon death.

The Deep Roots of Our Attitudes

Our nature and attitudes often have their roots in past lives. Thus, some people are naturally diehard optimists while others are hopeless pessimists.

As an example of the former, take the case of Arunima Sinha. In her youth, she was a sportswoman of moderate accomplishment. In November 2011, she was traveling by train from Lucknow to Delhi to participate in the National Games. Unfortunately, at night, robbers entered the train and began to ransack the passengers with abandon. Arunima, being of fiery spirit, put up a resistance. This invoked the wrath of the thieves, and to inject fear in other passengers, they took the harsh step of throwing her out of the moving train. Poor Arunima fell onto the parallel railway track. As luck would have it, at the same time a train was coming from the other side, and it went over Arunima's leg, shearing it below the knee.

The courageous girl lay on the track all night with one leg cut. In the morning, nearby villagers discovered her and took her to the nearest medical facility. When the news appeared in the media, it caused a national uproar. Arunima was airlifted to Delhi and treated at the All India Institute of Medical Sciences (AIIMS). An immediate surgery was performed, and she was given an artificial limb. That was the end of her volleyball career.

Arunima's dreams of entering the national women's volleyball team had been dashed to the ground by the cruel hand of fate. But such was her indomitable spirit that it refused to be suppressed. She said to herself, 'I cannot succeed in volleyball, but I will still succeed in life.' She soon learned that Bachendri Pal, the first Indian woman to climb Mount Everest, was conducting classes in mountain climbing. Arunima decided that this would be the field in which she'd make her mark. She completed the course on mountain climbing, and in May 2013, attempted to scale the highest peak of the world.

On the way up to Mount Everest, the party was caught in a snowstorm, and the loose snow caused her artificial leg to come off. Arunima sat on the snow holding her leg in her hand, while the climbers in the line behind her urged to be given way. She quietly moved to the side, alone in the snow, and then gathering courage, put back her leg and continued the ascent joining the rest of the party. On 21 May 2013, she became the first woman amputee in the world to climb Mount Everest.

When we hear tales of such courage and determination, we wonder what is the source of valour of people like Arunima? Did she develop all her inner strength and courage in this life itself? That seems highly improbable since she possessed it from youth.

At the other end of the spectrum, we also come across examples of people who have a hopelessly pessimistic attitude. Their mind does not believe anything good can ever happen to them, and their pessimism seems to work like a wish-fulfilling prophecy, as they move from debacle to disaster in their life.

YOU TESTED POSITIVE FOR BEING NEGATIVE

This wide spectrum of human attitudes is not the result of mental thought patterns developed in just one life. They are the consequence of images and impressions in the subconscious from many past lifetimes. How, then, can such a vast and deep mind be improved and controlled?

Ongoing Self-Talk in Our Mind

We have seen the subconscious basis of conscious attitudes. The subconscious stores data, retrieves it, and passes it to the conscious. It has the potential of a double-edged sword. It can be our worst foe and cripple our personality with its debilitating attitudes. But it can also be our foremost benefactor and provide inner strength through never-say-die positive attitudes.

The problem is that the subconscious can only create sentiments and feelings, but it cannot reason logically. And that is why it gets us into trouble with illogical fears, likes, and dislikes. If we wish to make the subconscious our friend and partner in life, we must be very careful of the inputs we consciously pass to it. **The intellect and the conscious mind must train the subconscious and diligently seed it with positive assertions.**

For instance, if we wish to programme our subconscious with positivity, we need to consciously seed it with positive thoughts and prevent contaminating it with negative thoughts. If we wish our subconscious to help us become fearless, we ought to indoctrinate it with thoughts, such as: 'God is with me. There is nothing to fear.' or 'He takes care of all the living beings in the world. Why will He not take care of me?'

This brings us to the topic of self-talk, which is the act of consciously speaking to ourselves within our mind. The self-talk gets passed to the subconscious. One person repetitively thinks, 'I am sick ... I am sick ... I am sick.' Consequently, the subconscious becomes convinced of the state of ill-health. It then repeatedly tells the conscious mind that it is feeling unwell.

Another person repeatedly thinks, 'I am getting well ... I am getting well ... I am getting well.' Accordingly, the subconscious firmly begins to believe that the body is well. These feel-good thoughts are then supplied abundantly to the conscious mind.

Some people ask the question: Do we talk to ourselves? Well, I have seen people speaking to their billiard balls: 'Come on ... just a few inches more. Aah ... you did it!' When people talk to billiard balls, what is so surprising about speaking to themselves?

I was once staying in a devotee's home. Suddenly a commotion began in the room upstairs. I went up to see what the matter was and was amused to see the person's three-year-old son playing with his toys. He was having a gala time and was speaking to himself all the while. Now, as adults, if in the same fashion, we spoke out aloud to ourselves, we would be considered insane. It is crazy people who mumble to themselves while walking down a street. To avoid such a label, we have learned to engage in self-talk silently.

For example, let us say you are talking to someone. Alongside with the discussion, you engage in self-talk, 'This person is speaking too much ... I am bored now ... He does not know what he is talking about.' This is the constant mental chatter that our conscious mind indulges in. And our subconscious unintentionally becomes programmed by it.

Using Self-Talk to Programme Our Mind

If our self-talk is negative and pessimistic, it permeates down to the subconscious and our personality becomes cynical and miserable. It is not uncommon for our inner voice to be our own worst enemy. It is the tormentor in the head that is incessantly punishing us and draining us of vital energy. Instead, if we use the power of affirmations to our benefit, we can programme our psyche in very positive ways.

Sports persons and athletes have always exploited the power of self-talk. For them, a hundredth of a second improvement in their performance can mean the difference between a silver and a gold medal. Consequently, they strive to bring their body-mind-intellect to a state of peak performance. To accomplish it, they repeatedly speak to themselves.

The legendary Muhammad Ali's indoctrination of himself with 'I am the greatest' is well-known. However, his is not the only example of self-talk amongst champions. Practically all sports champs at the higher competitive levels stimulate themselves with self-talk such as 'you need to relax', 'stay calm', 'stay focused', and so on. They do it either verbally or silently in the mind.

The first Olympic Games of modern times were held in 1896, in Athens. However, until 1954, nobody had run the mile in less than four minutes. It was considered an impossibility and various reasons were attributed why it could not be done. Some said that the heart was not strong enough—if exerted so much, the heart would burst. Others said that the lungs were too small for it—they could not supply the oxygen to sustain the effort.

Then came a medical student, Roger Bannister. He refused to believe that the four-minute barrier was unbreakable. His self-talk was 'I can do it .... I can do it.' His subconscious became programmed accordingly, and consequently, on 6 May 1954, with minimal training, he ran the mile in 3 minutes 59.4 seconds.

The miracle that followed Roger Bannister's achievement was astonishing. Just forty-five days later, his competitor, John Landy, ran a mile in 3 minutes 58 seconds. The matter did not stop there. In the same year, 29 runners broke the four-minute barrier. The next year, 237 runners clocked the sub-four-minute mile. What had suddenly changed? Roger Bannister's feat had altered the self-talk of all middle distance runners to 'It can be done .... It can be done.'

Deliberate self-talk for the purpose of programming the mind is called 'positive affirmation'. It capitalises on the power of repetition. When a message is iterated again and again, it goes deep within and is internalised. In mind management, positive affirmations have a significant role to play. We can use it to develop a positive personality, full of optimism, faith, courage, perseverance, and purpose. Some positive affirmations we can use are:

1) *I have infinite potential for growth.*
2) *The universe has a great plan for me.*
3) *God's grace is upon me. I will surely succeed.*
4) *I am protected by my divine Father. There is nothing to fear. There is abundance in the universe, and I will always have enough.*
5) *My body is in good health. The organs are healthy and well.*
6) *Every cell in my body is sparkling with joy and bliss.*
7) *I will focus on the effort without worrying about the results.*
8) *Whatever happens will be for the good.*

9) *I can do it. I will succeed. The goal is almost achieved.*
10) *My work is very important. I am trying to please God through it.*
11) *I have received so much from God. I must give back through devotion.*

Positive affirmation is thus carefully selected self-talk that moulds our subconscious in the manner we desire. Let us now understand how to use this tool to attain loving devotion to God.

Chanting the Names of God

In the previous chapter, we had learned that success in karm yog requires absorbing our mind in the Lord. But how can we develop such loving devotion? To accomplish this, positive affirmation is a powerful tool. The Vedic scriptures present it in the form of *japa* (chanting the Names of God). **Chanting the Name is a very convenient way of remembering God since it can be done anywhere and everywhere**—while walking, talking, sitting, eating, or while engaged in any other task.

As we chant His Name, we urge the mind to think lovingly of Him. Repeatedly, the mind is forced to return from its wanderings and think of God. In the various Bhakti traditions of India, it is made the basis of divine contemplation. Thus, the Ramayan states:

brahma rāma teṅ nāmu baṛa, bara dāyaka bara dāni

'God's Name is bigger than God Himself, in terms of its utility to the souls.' Lord Krishna also refers to japa in the Bhagavad Gita:

yajñānāṁ japa-yajño 'smi (10.25)

'Amongst all kinds of sacrifices, I am the chanting of the divine Names.'

Yajna is the act of dedicating ourselves to the Supreme. Chanting the holy Names of God is the simplest and most superior of all yajnas. It is called japa yajna. In this verse, Shree Krishna explains that taking His name is the highest sacrifice one can perform.

In fire yajnas, a number of rules are applicable, all of which need to be meticulously followed. However, in japa yajna, there are no rules. It can be done anywhere and at any time, and it is more purifying than the other forms of yajnas. That is why japa was widely recommended 500 years ago during the Bhakti movement in India. Chaitanya Mahaprabhu said:

nāmnām akāri bahudhā nija sarva śhaktis
tatrārpitā niyamitaḥ smaraṇe na kālah
(*Śhikṣhāṣhṭaka* verse 2)

'O Shree Krishna! You have innumerable Names, and in each of these You have filled all Your energies. You have laid no rules for chanting these Names (and hence, anyone can chant them).'

God has numerous names, and we can utter any of them e.g. 'Radhey Shyam', 'Sita Ram', 'Namah Shivaya', 'Jai Mata di', and many others. When we repeatedly chant any divine Name, it sends devotional prompts to the subconscious, attaching it to the Lord.

Some people take the help of rosary beads to do japa. The downside of using rosary beads is that the chanting becomes mechanical. It turns into a formality of completing a certain number of rotations of the beads. A better way is to chant with every breath instead of the beads. Jagadguru Kripalu-ji Maharaj states:

śhwāsa jaba khīṇcho to 'rā' kahu, manahiṅ mana te pyāre
śhwāsa jaba chhoḍo to kahu 'dhey,' dhyāna bhī karu pyāre
(*Sādhanā Karu Pyāre*)

'Dear one! Every time you inhale, say 'Rā' in your mind. And every time you exhale, say 'dhey', all the while meditating on God.'

Also, there is no need to take any mantra initiation in the ear from a guru. The Supreme Lord has innumerable Names and we are free to chant any of them. Since the Lord is seated in His Name, no guru mantra can be bigger than the Name of the Lord.

We have seen the benefits of positive affirmations in purifying the mind right down to its subconscious roots. We have also seen how chanting the Names of God helps absorb the mind in the Lord. However, you will be surprised to know that there is yet another technique, a thousand times more powerful than affirmations, and that is the methodology of visualisation and positive imagery. We will discuss this next.

SUMMARY OF THE MAIN POINTS

- Just as we change clothes every morning, the soul too changes bodies upon death. When the soul departs from the body, the mind goes with it. Hence, the mind continues with the soul from past lifetimes.
- The mind has two aspects : the conscious and the subconscious.
- The subconscious has the potential of a double-edged sword. It can either cripple our personality with debilitating attitudes, or it can provide immense support through never-say-die attitudes.
- Thus, if we wish to make our subconscious our friend and partner for success in life, we must be very careful of the inputs we allow to pass into the conscious mind.
- Self-talk is what we speak to ourselves within our mind. These become the messages we repeatedly pass from the conscious to the subconscious. Such kind of self-talk is called 'positive affirmation'. We can use it to develop a positive personality, full of optimism, faith, courage, perseverance, and purpose.
- Vedic scriptures present positive affirmations in the form of japa or the chanting of the Names of God. In the various bhakti traditions of Indian, japa is the basis of contemplation. But an even more powerful tool than japa is visualisation.

VISUALISATION AND ROOP DHYAN MEDITATION

In the previous chapter, we saw how most of our attitudes are not consciously chosen emotional responses to situations. Rather, they have their origins in the subconscious mind. This is why we must strive to purify the inner vistas of our mind to its deepest depths. We discussed positive affirmations as an effective tool for accomplishing it. We also saw the benefits of 'chanting' as a tool for developing love for God. Let us now discuss a method that is many times more powerful. This is the technique of visualisation.

A Picture is Worth a Thousand Words

We all have heard the above adage. It states that just a single image is sufficient to convey a complicated concept which would typically require many words to describe. The reason is that we are habituated to thinking in terms of images.

For example, whenever we wish to think of a car, we bring its image to our mind. This is because the first time we learned the concept of a car, as children, it was with an image. Consequently, when we search for our car in the parking lot, we do not look at the license plates. Rather, we have an image of our car in mind, and we compare the vehicles we see against that image. When it matches, we say, 'Aha! There is my car.'

A picture not only conveys ideas more effectively, it also creates a greater impact upon the mind. A Chinese saying states: *băi wén bù rú yī jiàn.* 'Hearing something a hundred times is not better than seeing it once.'

Napoleon Bonaparte was also reputed to have said: *Un bon croquis vaut mieux qu'un long discours.* 'A good sketch is better than a long speech.'

The mind also remembers images more easily than words. Let us say, that in the morning you think, 'I need to call my friend at 6 p.m.,' but you are worried that by evening, you may forget. How can you improve the chances of your remembering to make the phone call?

One way is to take the help of mental imagery. On the screen of your mind, visualise yourself on the phone. Now expand the image of the phone handset to make it giant-sized. Let it remain in your mind for a few seconds. The image will go deeper in your memory than words would have and your chances of forgetting the phone appointment will reduce tremendously. Consider another example.

Most of us make New Year's resolutions at the beginning of the year. We conceptualise our resolves in words, such as 'I will get up at 5 a.m. every day,' 'I will cut down on eating unhealthy food,' 'I will do thirty minutes of yoga every day,' and so on. Often, we take a step further and write down our New Year's resolutions in our diaries. However, the problem is that the diaries are rarely opened, and within a few weeks, the resolutions are forgotten. Instead, if we vividly picture them in the mind, and allow those images to sink in; our chances of remembering them in future will increase manifold.

The mind uses both involuntary and voluntary imagery while thinking. Modern psychology is eager to understand how our mind uses images in its thinking process. While they ponder over this phenomenon, let us focus on using the powerful affinity of the mind for visuals to our advantage.

The Technique of Visualisation

Visualisation taps the human mind's propensity for thinking in terms of pictures. It is the process of consciously creating images, with the eyes open or closed, for producing the

CLOSE YOUR EYES. NOW VISUALIZE SITTING ON THE WALL AND NOT FALLING OFF

desired beneficial effect. In it, the conscious mind forms images that will create a beneficial impact on the subconscious. Personal coaches use guided imagery to help their clients become motivated, optimistic, or relaxed, by helping them change their inner conception of situations and outcomes.

The technique of visualisation is of two types: *process visualisation* and *outcome visualisation.*

1. Process Visualisation entails imagining the steps required to accomplish a work and then mentally practising them to achieve competence. Interestingly, research has shown that the brain activity during visualisation is similar to that during actual physical practice. A study looking at brain patterns in weightlifters found that when they lifted hundreds of pounds, the patterns activated were almost like those when they only imagined carrying weights.

Competitive sports in the international arena demands peak performance of the body and perfect attitude of the mind. Thus, athletes and sportspersons extensively use process visualisation to enhance their performance. Let us hear from the greatest golfer of all time:

The legendary golfer, Jack Nicklaus, cites visualisation as his topmost secret of success. He states: 'I never hit a shot, not even in practice, without having a very sharp, in-focus picture of it in my head.' He explains the concept further: 'First, I see the ball where I want it to finish, nice and white, and sitting up high on the bright green grass. Then the scene quickly changes, and I see the ball going there—its path, trajectory, and shape, even its behaviour on landing. Then there is a sort of fade-out, and the next scene shows me making the kind of swing that will turn the previous images into reality.'

Visual practice done in the mind works because the neurons in the brain interpret images as equivalent to real-life action. While visualising an action, the brain generates impulses akin to actually performing the movement. This creates neural pathways in the brain leading to learned behaviour. Amazingly, all this occurs without the physical activity actually being performed.

Dr John F. Murray, a Florida-based sports psychologist, writes, 'Imagery is practice but you don't have to pay for the court. It's just minus the last step when the brain signals the muscle to move. You're re-creating an experience without the external stimuli.' Dr Murray makes tennis players visualise a troublesome aspect of their game. After seeing that problem once, they follow up with repeated images of the move, performed perfectly

Visualisation is a way to become 'unconsciously competent'.

2. Outcome Visualisation entails imagining yourself achieving the goal. In it, you create a mental image of the desired outcome and feel the accompanying emotions of success, happiness, and fulfilment. Arnold Schwarzenegger, five times Mr Universe, attributed his success to outcome visualisation:

The first time Schwarzenegger won the Mr Universe title, he was asked by reporters whether he was surprised by his victory. He replied that he was not surprised in the least, for he had visualised standing on the victory stand thousands of times in his mind. Regarding his use of mental imagery, he said, 'I never set limits or created mental barriers. I imagined my biceps as big as mountain peaks when I did my curling exercises. This visualisation process was essential if I was to gain the kind of mass and size I needed to win the Mr Olympia contest ....'

Why is the technique of outcome visualisation so effective? It works so well because it is not possible to consciously control all hundred billion neurons of the brain, the attitude of the mind, and the coordination of limbs for peak performance. But when images are held in the conscious or subconscious mind, they naturally send signals to the body and mind to work in the manner required for the task.

A very inspiring story about the powerful results that accrue from visualisation is from the life of Natan Sharansky. He was born in the Soviet Union in 1948. In 1978, he was sentenced by the communist regime to thirteen years of forced labour. In prison, he retained his sanity by playing chess in his mind. He would visualise himself competing against the world chess champion and defeating him. As a result of an international campaign by his wife, he was finally released in 1986.

He then went to live in Israel. In 1996, the reigning world chess champion, Gary Kasparov, visited Israel. In a simultaneous exhibition match, Sharansky defeated Kasparov. When asked about his shock victory, he said he was not astonished for he had defeated Kasparov thousands of times in his mind!

This technique now finds application in the field of therapeutics. For example, if one steadily holds the image of oneself as being healthy and well, it favourably affects the physical processes and mental activities in the direction of wellness. Here is a testimony of its effectiveness from one of the most eminent yogis of modern times:

Paramahansa Yogananda, one of the first swamis to come to the US from India, used this technique to reduce his weight. He mentions in his famous book, Autobiography of a Yogi, *that when he began his spiritual charitable work in America, he realised he was overweight and needed to lose a few pounds. He held a slimmer image of himself in his mind, along with the thought that he wished to reduce his weight, and soon the body responded by becoming trimmer.*

In this way, visualisation is an even more powerful technique than affirmation for influencing our subconscious mind. In light of this fact, one wonders if there is a way of harnessing its potential for absorbing the mind in God as well? We next discuss how to leverage the process of visualisation for developing love for God.

Using Visualisation to Nurture Devotion

In the last chapter, we discussed the technique of chanting the Names of God. Such chanting, or jāpa, has been widely recommended by the Bhakti saints of India as a means of bhakti. However, chanting must be accompanied with devotional remembrance or else it becomes a mechanical recitation of words. For example, if we are chanting the Names of Lord

Krishna, we must also remember His personality. Sage Patanjali described the proper style for japa:

taj japastadartha bhāvanam (*Yog Darśhan* 1.28)

'Whatever japa you do, create the corresponding sentiment in your mind as well.'

But this is not as easy as it sounds. People often complain that though they chant the divine Names, their mind continues to wander in the world. They are at a loss to figure out how to focus the mind on God.

The reason for the wandering of the mind is its habit of interacting with forms and shapes. In endless past lifetimes, wherever we attached our mind, it would cling to forms and images. Now, in devotion, if the Name of God is all we offer to the mind, it will not experience the charming attraction required for deep absorption. However, if we add a divine image along with the chanting, the mind will get a tangible basis for devotion.

That is also how we remember people. If you think of your spouse, what do you remember? Your spouse's name or image? Image, of course! It is the most natural way of bringing your spouse to your mind. The sentiments may be further enhanced by recalling your spouse's qualities or activities, but the image is what forms the basis.

The same principle applies to the divine realm as well. We **use the image of the Lord as the basis for our meditation. This is called *Roop Dhyan*.** For example, if you are chanting the Names of Lord Ram, bring His image before your eyes and then chant. This will immediately bring your mind to focus upon the Lord. Now, with the image of the Lord in front, you can then nurture your devotion by cultivating divine sentiments towards Him.

We will discuss various aspects of Roop Dhyan meditation in the sections ahead and see their efficacy as a form of spiritual practice. Let us start by addressing three questions that people often ask me about this most powerful technique.

Question 1. How Can We Visualise the Supreme Without Having Seen Him?

Upon hearing about Roop Dhyan meditation, people raise a doubt: 'I've seen my husband, wife, son, and daughter, so I am able to visualise them. But how will I visualise God whom I have never seen?'

Actually, the question is incorrect. Tell me, the first time that you went to some wonderful place--let's say, the Taj Mahal, the Eiffel Tower, or the Statue of Liberty—had you ever seen it before? Of course not! If it was your first visit, how could you have seen it earlier? Then, without any prior experience of it, how did you develop the yearning to see it?

The answer is that you heard how wonderful it was from people who had been there, and you also saw its pictures in books. Similarly, the saints who have seen God inform us that He is the very epitome of beauty. The scriptures also describe His personality as all-attractive and enchanting. From what we have heard and read, can we not create the desire to love and see Him? Definitely we can, just as we did in the world! Therefore, begin your practice of Roop Dhyan without having seen God.

Besides, having darshan of God is the fruit of our sadhana. We cannot demand the fruit without having put in the effort. No student says, 'Give me the post-graduate degree certificate after which I will begin studying from grade one.' If any student makes such an absurd demand, parents and teachers will say, 'That is impossible. First work hard day and night for seventeen years and then you will get the joy of being felicitated with a post-graduate degree.'

IF I PAY YOU DOUBLE, CAN YOU MAKE ME SKIP PRACTICE AND GET STRAIGHT TO PERFECT?

Likewise, no gardener says, 'Let me first have the juicy mango fruit and later I will plant the tree.' If they do, they will surely be told, 'That can never happen. You must first plant the seed and water it regularly. When the plant emerges, nurture it with fertiliser, water, and sunlight. Then carefully protect the sapling from cows. Only after five years, will the tree bear the fruit you desire.'

In the same manner, in devotion to God as well, we must first practise meditation without seeing His divine form. Only later, after becoming God-realised, will we have the good fortune of actually seeing Him with our eyes.

Question 2. Does God Possess a Form or is He a Formless Light?

The answer is that the Supreme—being all-powerful and infinite—is not limited to our finite conceptions of Him. Therefore:

- If we say that God cannot possess a form, then we are limiting Him.
- If we say God cannot be formless, then also we are limiting Him.

The infinite and all-powerful Lord is both. He possesses infinite forms and is also formless. Both these perspectives are endorsed in the Vedic scriptures. At the same time, these scriptures also state that worship of the formless is difficult and problematic. The Bhagavad Gita says:

kleśho 'dhikataras teṣhām avyaktāsakta-chetasām
avyaktā hi gatir duḥkhaṁ dehavadbhir avāpyate (12.5)

'For those whose minds are attached to the unmanifest, the path of realisation is full of tribulations. Worship of the unmanifest is exceedingly difficult for embodied beings.'

Thus, the easiest way for bringing the Supreme Divine Personality to your mind is to contemplate upon His image. Meditation upon any of the innumerable forms of God is also devotionally sweeter than meditation upon formless light.

Question 3. How Can the Material Mind Visualise the Lord's Divine Form?

The above objection is often raised by devotees who worship God in His formless aspect. They opine that meditation on the form is a material meditation while meditation on the formless light is transcendental meditation. They criticise worshippers of the personal form of God for creating an image of Him with their mind. They say that the mind is made from maya, so whatever form it conjectures is also material. Thus, the form of God we visualise with our mind is just our imagination—it is not His divine form.

It is indeed true that the form we make with our mind is a material form. But the fact is that worshippers of the formless aspect of God are doing no better. They are also merely focusing on a light created by the mind—it is not really the divine light of God. The Ramayan states: *go gochara jahañ lagi mana jāī, so saba māyā jānehu bhāī.* 'Wherever the mind can go is all the realm of maya.' In other words, as long as we have a material mind, divine meditation is not possible—whether on the formless or on the personal form.

How, then, can the material mind visualise the image of the Supreme Almighty, who is beyond the realm of maya? The *Kenopaniṣhad* states:

yanmanasā na manute yenāhurmanomatam,
tadeva brahma tvaṁ viddhi nedaṁ yadidamupāsate

(verse 1.5)

'The mind cannot think of Him; it is by His power that the mind thinks.' When we reach the state of *mām ekaṁ śharaṇaṁ vraja*, or complete surrender, we receive His grace. Then our mind becomes divine and we do not need to imagine His form. We truly see Him—as He is—standing before us, in His original form!

Therefore, actual meditation on the divine can only happen when, by the grace of God, our mind becomes divine. Until then, we have to meditate upon the imagined form. Do not worry that the image of the Lord you make with your mind is material. Use that image to increase your love for Him. But create divine sentiments towards the object of your meditation. Those divine sentiments will purify the mind.

Presently in our meditation, there is no stipulated form that we must focus upon. We are free to choose any form of the Lord we consider attractive. We also have the liberty to meditate on any deity or picture of God. Alternately, we can also create any form of His in our mind. The important point is to keep increasing our love for Him.

Roop Dhyan meditation, the practice of visualisation of the image of God, can be practised in conjunction with other devotional techniques of meditation. These meditative practices help absorb the mind even more deeply in the divine realm and increase our love for God. We will now discuss four such meditational techniques.

The Technique of Meditation Upon Divine Qualities

Visualisation is more effective with meditation on divine virtues. How does that help? Our mind is naturally drawn to attractive qualities wherever we see them. For example, it is natural to think:

- *That lady is so graceful and carries herself with such elegance.*
- *He is so knowledgeable. I am charmed by his immense wisdom.*
- *She is such a simple person. I am drawn by the openness and integrity of her personality.*

Qualities like these obviously appeal to our mind. The Supreme Divine Personality is an ocean of such qualities. Sage Ved Vyas states:

yo vā anantasya guṇān anantān
anukramiṣhyan sa tu bāla-buddhiḥ
rajāṁsi bhūmer gaṇayet kathañchit
kālena naivākhila-śhakti-dhāmnaḥ

(Shreemad Bhagavatam 11.4.2)

'Those who think they can count the innumerable qualities of the Lord possess a childish intellect. We may succeed in counting the grains of sands on the crust of the earth, but we can never completely enumerate God's infinite virtues.'

When such is the nature of God, then why is our mind not drawn to Him? The reason is very simple: we have not pondered deeply and sufficiently about His wonderful attributes. The more we contemplate on God's divine virtues, the more our love for Him will grow.

In this manner, after visualising the Lord's form, we can imbue our meditation with His divine qualities. For example:

- *Lord Krishna's form is so enchanting. He is full of beauty.*
- *Lord Shiv is so kind and merciful. He is ever eager to grace the souls of the world.*
- *Sita Ram are my eternal relatives and are waiting with open arms to embrace me.*
- *I am indebted to my guru for the divine knowledge he bestows upon me.*

When we contemplate upon the divine qualities of God, not only do they absorb the mind, but our meditation also becomes sweeter and more blissful.

If you want my personal guidance in this process, you can join the Daily Sadhana site (*www.mydailysadhana.org*) where you will have access to a variety of meditations recorded by me.

The Technique of Meditation Upon Divine Pastimes

We can also meditate upon the *leelas* or pastimes of God. These too play a big role in diverting our mind in His direction. In the Indian culture, people have grown up hearing narratives, enactments, dances, and bhajans based upon the various leelas of the different avatars of God, and hence, they connect so easily with them. This was amply demonstrated when the Ramayan series was first aired on Doordarshan, the Indian national TV channel, at prime time on Sunday mornings in 1987. Entire markets would become empty and streets would be deserted, as if under curfew, as people sat in their homes glued to their

TV sets relishing the leelas of Lord Ram. This fascination of the mind for God's pastimes can easily be used to charm our mind towards Him.

We can visualise His leelas as we wish. There is no need to limit ourselves to the few leelas described in the Puranas. Instead, we can envisage them as we like. For instance:

- *Lord Ram and Mother Sita are coming to my home. I am welcoming Them with flower garlands and ārati. They are sitting in my drawing room and accepting my humble food offering.*
- *Radha Krishna are sitting under a beautiful tree in the garden of my house. The gopis are singing and dancing for Them. I am standing by the side and watching.*
- *Radha Krishna are sitting on a swing, while clouds are gathered above, and a pleasant breeze is blowing. I am standing behind the swing and pushing it gently for Their pleasure.*

The idea is to absorb the mind in the activities and pastimes of God in a very natural way. When we do this, devotion does not remain artificial or contrived, rather it comes effortlessly and easily.

Devotional remembrance can be further enhanced by *sevā* (service) and this too can be performed in the mind (*mānasī sevā*).

The Technique of Serving God in the Mind

Divine love is all about giving and manifests in the desire to serve. Thus, devotees traditionally serve the deities they worship in various ways, such as bathing, clothing, decorating, and doing pooja (worship). These too can be performed in the mind as mānasī sevā.

Mānasī sevā is simple and does not have any of the traditional constraints. For service of the physical deity, you might need flowers for offering, and if you live in a snowbound place or an apartment, flowers may not be easily available. Further, if you wish to put a diamond necklace on the deity, you may not have the finances to afford it. But the service that we offer in the mind has none of these constraints. Simply imagine preparing a garland of the most exquisite roses and offering it. Or visualise placing a necklace, with a diamond even larger than the Kohinoor, around Shree Krishna's neck.

Travelling is always a problem with the physical deity. One is nagged by the question whether to carry the deity along or to leave it behind. Leaving it behind without worship often causes uneasiness in the devotee's heart. But carrying the deity in the luggage has its own set of problems, for then one is forced to pack it with shoes and undergarments in the limited baggage that airlines permit. All such issues are avoided when we visualise an image in our mind. Whenever we have free time, we can close our eyes and absorb ourselves in serving the Lord—massaging His feet, feeding Him, fanning Him, worshipping Him, and so on. A poet described it well:

dil meṅ basī hai yār kī tasvīr, jab chāhā sir jhukāyā dekh liyā

'In my mind resides the image of my Soul-Beloved. Whenever I wish, I lower my eyes and see Him.'

The important point is that just like physical seva, mānasī sevā also purifies the mind. A beautiful example from the leelas of Lord Krishna illustrates this concept.

When Krishna left Vrindavan and came to Mathura, he killed Kansa, the demon king, and liberated His parents. At that time, His mother Devaki, who was meeting her child after eleven years, sat Him in her lap and hugged Him tightly. Krishna's father, Vasudev, reminded Devaki of their resolve that they would only take Krishna in their lap after donating ten thousand cows in charity. However, Devaki's motherly love was so intense that she was not willing to listen to Vasudev's admonishment. Consequently, Vasudev decided to implement the vow himself. Since he did not have ten thousand cows or the resources to get them, he did the next best thing. He meditated on giving away the cows in his mind.

This may seem facile, but the fact is that **when we think noble thoughts of sacrifice and service, it naturally results in purification of the mind.** The Buddhist scriptures very beautifully explain this point. They emphasise that when we do good to others, we simultaneously do good to ourselves. This is because, before doing good, we bring noble sentiments to our mind. As a result, we elevate our own mind, thereby benefitting ourselves. And when we do bad to others, we end up doing bad to ourselves, because the bad sentiments create poison in our own mind. In other words, harbouring good thoughts purifies the mind while nurturing bad thoughts poisons it. Thus, if we cannot do good, the next best thing is to ***think*** of doing good.

The same principle applies to manasī sevā. The practice of serving God in the mind purifies the devotee just as physical sevā does. Let me tell you a lovely story illustrating this spiritual axiom.

There was once a trader who was devotional but very miserly. Wherever he got the opportunity, he would save his pennies, no matter what extent he had to go to do it. One day he attended satsang, and there he heard that all the pooja can also be performed in the mind. He thought this to be very convenient as the money spent in the worship paraphernalia would be saved.

The next day, he sat in meditation. He brought before him the image of his beloved Lord Krishna. Then, he gathered the water of all the holy rivers—Ganga, Yamuna, Narmada, Sindhu, and Kaveri—and began bathing Shree Krishna in his mind. He lovingly clothed and decorated the Lord. Then, he cooked a meal and fed Him with his own hands. The entire experience lasted an hour, and he enjoyed it thoroughly, relishing the feeling of closeness and intimacy with the Lord of his heart. He decided to do this service every day.

A year went by and his meditation became deeper. He would feel that the paraphernalia of worship was actually there as he did his daily pooja. One day, he was meditating upon preparing kheer (an Indian dessert). He boiled the rice in the milk and added some seasonings. Then, while meditating upon adding the kesar (saffron), he felt as if the entire kesar in the box had fallen into the milk. Now, kesar is very expensive and every strand of it is valuable. He hated the fact that money was being wasted here. Without realising that it was only in his meditation, he began picking the kesar out of the milk so that he may reuse it the next day.

God notes every thought that passes through our mind and had been noting the service that the trader would perform daily. Seeing his sincerity, Lord Krishna decided to bestow His grace. He manifested in His personal form before the trader and caught his hand. The trader's divine reverie broke. He opened his eyes and was astonished to see God before him. Lord Krishna chided him lovingly, 'You miser! Did you spend any of your father's inheritance in the kesar that you had to take it out?' The trader was thrilled to have darshan of the Lord.

This is a humorous story, but it highlights the powerful manner in which serving God and guru in the mind develops our loving sentiments for Them.

The Technique of Meditation in the Sentiment of Longing

Finally, there is a form of meditation even higher than all the ones previously discussed and that is *viraha dhyan* (meditation in longing). In this, we keep the image of the Lord in front of us and cultivate the longing for His divine darshan: 'When will that day come when He will actually manifest before me in His original divine form?'

Then, feeling humbled by our lack of purity and devotion, we cry out to God for His grace, with tears of love: 'My Lord, the fact that You are not revealing Yourself to me means that my mind is yet impure. I have tried my best to reach You and still not succeeded. My efforts are limited and full of defects. Now You please grace me with Your causeless mercy and consummate my sadhana.'

In viraha dhyan, we increase the longing of all our senses for God. Such longing for the Supreme Beloved is the very life of devotion. It increases our love for Him at every moment and leads to the experience called *viraha vedanā,* which is the pain in the heart while yearning for God. When that arises, it very quickly cleans the impurities in the heart making it a fit vessel for divine love.

Jagadguru Kripalu-ji Maharaj describes the viraha sentiment in his compositions:

de do aisī viraha vedanā miṭa jāye mama ahama chetana
aura adhika chamakegā sonā puni puni agini tapāne se

'O Shree Krishna! Make my heart such that it pines only for You. Such longing will kill my self-conceit and purify my heart, just as gold sparkles even more when it is repeatedly put in fire.'

Yogi Shree Krishna Prem expressed this sentiment very well when he said:

> The divine grace intervenes only when you are at the end of your tether, for then feeling lost, as you call out with every fibre of your being to save you from your shipwreck, His love answers your call, and your heart is flooded with love, His light knelling the doom of centuries of darkness.

Having discussed the various tools of mind management along with Roop Dhyan meditation, we are now in a position to set up our daily sadhana. We discuss this in the next and final chapter of this book.

SUMMARY OF THE MAIN POINTS

- Visualisations are more effective than positive self-talk and affirmations. A picture is worth a thousand wofds. A picture has a greater impact on the mind than words. The mind also remembers images more easily.
- Visualisation is the process of consciously creating images, with the eyes open or closed, for producing the desired beneficial effect.
- When we learn to meditate upon the image of God, we get a tangible basis for loving Him. This is Roop Dhyan meditation.
- The divine form of God can only be visualised when, after God-realisation, our mind becomes divine. Presently, we have to create a mental image of Him and develop divine sentiments.
- We can also meditate upon the qualities and divine pastimes of God.
- Manasi seva, is another powerful way of cultivating love for God.
- Viraha dhyan is meditation upon God in the sentiment of longing. It is the most powerful way of cultivating devotion.

SETTING UP YOUR DAILY SADHANA

A famous proverb states: 'Good ideas are a dime a dozen, but they are not worth a single nickel if they are not put into practice'. In the previous nine chapters, we discussed extremely powerful tools for managing the mind. But unless these are applied practically, mere theoretical knowledge of the techniques is worthless. What is the difference between an educated drug addict and an uneducated one? Not much, really. They may differ in their knowledge but are alike in their behaviour. Therefore, after learning the wonderful theory of mind management, we now need to apply it in our daily life.

This will require practice. Mastery in any field comes from consistent, disciplined, and steady practice. One who swims in the local pool once a week on Saturday evenings does not become an Olympic swimming champion. Those who practice for several hours every day, enhancing their skills and strength, are the ones who win the gold medals. For spiritual excellence as well, training is essential. This training must be done under the guidance of a guru, which is the next topic we will discuss.

The Need for a Guru

It is a well-known fact in corporate and professional life that the easiest way to leapfrog your career is to find a mentor who can personally guide and coach you. Such a mentor has first-hand experience of the path, having 'been there and done that' as the expression goes. Because of the depth of experience, your mentor can easily teach you the knowledge that would otherwise take you decades to accumulate. In the field of sports too, the value of a good mentor is universally recognised. Similarly, the guru is a spiritual mentor who guides us on the journey to inner perfection.

The word 'Guru' consists of two syllables—*gu* and *ru*. *Gu* means 'darkness' and *ru* means 'one who destroys'. Thus, the guru is the personality who destroys the darkness of ignorance from within us and brings us into the light of divine knowledge.

All the Vedic scriptures declare in unison that divine knowledge is received through the medium of the guru:

tadvijñānārthaṁ sagurumevābhigachchhet
samitpāniḥ śhrotriyaṁ bhramhaniṣhṭham
(*Muṇḍakopaniṣhad* 1.2.12)

'To know the Absolute Truth, approach a guru who knows the scriptures and is practically situated on the platform of God-realisation.'

tasmād guruṁ prapadyeta jijñāsuḥ śhreya uttamam
śhābde pare cha niṣhṇātaṁ brahmaṇy upaśhamāśhrayam
(Bhagavatam 11.3.21)

'Seekers of the Truth should surrender themselves to a spiritual master who has understood the conclusion of the scriptures and taken complete shelter of God, leaving aside all material considerations.'

tad viddhi praṇipātena paripraśhnena sevayā
upadekṣhyanti te jñānaṁ jñāninas tattva-darśhinaḥ
(Bhagavad Gita 4.34)

'Learn the truth by approaching a spiritual master. Inquire from him with reverence and render service unto him. Such an enlightened saint can impart knowledge unto you because he has seen the truth.'

guru binu bhava nidhi tarai na koī,
jauṅ biranchi sankara sama hoī (Ramayan)

'Not even the most elevated of spiritual aspirants can cross over the material ocean without the grace of the guru.'

As children, the education we received in school was also through the medium of a teacher. We had no idea what ABC ... looked like until we were taught. On the spiritual path, the guru is even more necessary since spiritual knowledge is not immediately perceptible. Further, in its practical application, we encounter many doubts and difficulties. For their resolution too, a teacher is necessary.

But there is a difference between the material and spiritual teacher. While the material teacher requires theoretical knowledge of the subject, the spiritual teacher must have both theoretical knowledge and practical realisation. To find such a guru is one of the biggest spiritual blessings. However, if we have not found a guru as yet, we should not wait. We should begin the journey with whatever knowledge we have gathered. In future, when we become eligible for it, God will connect us with our spiritual mentor.

I was blessed to have the benefit of personal guidance from a guru who was honoured not only as *Jagadguru* (spiritual master of the world) but also as *Jagadguruttam* (supreme among all Jagadgurus). The theoretical knowledge and practical illumination I received from him is what I am sharing here. Accordingly, let us now discuss how to accomplish spiritual mastery through daily practice.

The Importance of Sadhana in Seclusion

All day long, we live in and interact with a worldly environment. Material activities, people, and conversations all tend to increase the worldliness of the mind. Despite our best intentions, the distractions of the world sweep away our progress and soil our mind again. Therefore, in order to elevate and purify the mind, we need to dedicate some time for secluded sadhana (spiritual practice) on a daily basis.

Consider the example of milk. When mixed with water, it cannot retain its undiluted identity. However, if the milk is kept apart from water, converted into yogurt, and then churned to extract butter, it becomes unmixable. It can now challenge the water, 'I will sit on your head and float; you can do nothing to me for I have become butter.'

Our mind is like milk and the world is like water. In contact with the world, the mind gets distracted with worldliness and cannot retain divine consciousness. But an environment of seclusion blocks distraction and becomes conducive for focusing the mind on God. Once sufficient absorption in the Supreme has been achieved, then we can even challenge the world, and say, 'I will live amidst all the dualities of maya but remain untouched by them.' This elevated state is reached through sadhana in isolation.

The Bhagavad Gita emphasises such sadhana

vivikta sevī laghv-āśhī (18.52)

'Practise in a secluded place; control your diet.'

The Bible also states:

> 'When thou prayest, enter thy closet and lock thy door.' (Matthew 6:6)

Thus, in our daily schedule, we should allocate some time for sadhana in solitude. Shutting ourselves out from the world, we should practice meditation, contemplation, reflection, and devotion. This will help purify the mind and fill it with noble thoughts and aspirations.

After practising in quiet for an hour, for the rest of the day, we can work in divine consciousness, using the technique of karm yog as explained in chapter 7. In this manner, we will be able to sustain the elevated state of consciousness gathered during the daily sadhana all day long.

Let us now systematically discuss how sadhana is to be done.

Common Questions on the Practice of Sadhana

There are some ubiquitous questions regarding daily sadhana. These have been listed here along with their answers.

Q) In the turmoil of our everyday duties, how is it possible to devote time for sadhana?

A) It is not that we do not have time for sadhana in our daily lives. Rather, we do not realise its importance. The day we appreciate the dire need for improving the quality of our mind and thoughts, we will find that there is no shortage of time.

Q) On a daily basis, how long should I do sadhana?

A) The scriptures instruct us to do it for one-tenth of our time. It is the same rule that applies to wealth:

nyāyopārjita vittasya daśhamānśhena dhīmataḥ
kartavyo viniyogaśhcha īśhwaraprītyarthameva cha
(*Skanda Purāṇ*)

'Earn your wealth by just and legal means. Then, take out one-tenth of it and give it away in charity, in a manner that will please God.' The act of charity purifies our attitude towards wealth. Without such purification, wealth gets lost in court cases and doctors' bills.

Similarly, God has given us twenty-four hours in a day. We must dedicate one-tenth for spiritual practice which amounts to roughly two hours every day. Nevertheless, if two hours is too demanding, let us resolve to dedicate one hour, daily. But we must firmly commit to at least that much time for spiritual practice. Else, mere reading or hearing of even the most sublime wisdom will not bring about the inner transformation we seek.

Q) What is the best time for sadhana?

A) The ideal period of the day for spiritual practice is the early morning hours. After waking up, our mind is fresh and empty, so it is easy to take it towards God. Later, during the day, as we interact with the world, our mind gets filled with distracting impressions, and it becomes more challenging to absorb it in meditation. That is why the two morning hours before sunrise are considered the best for sadhana. This is the last portion of the night and is also referred to as *Brahma Muhūrt*, or 'The time for God'. The scriptures say: *brahme muhūrte uttiṣhṭhet.* 'Wake up by Brahma Muhūrt and do your sadhana.'

However, if our work or home commitments do not allow us to spare the morning hours, we can allocate some other time for it. And if a single long slot is not available, we can even split it into two smaller slots. We can customise our daily schedule to better suit our unique requirements.

Q) What posture should we adopt when we sit for sadhana?

A) The particular posture we adopt is not important. There are a number of meditative asanas (postures) such as *padmāsan, ardha padmāsan, dhyānvīr āsan, siddhāsan,* and *sukhāsan* described in the *Haṭha Yog Pradīpikā*. We may adopt any posture in which we can comfortably sit, without moving, during the period of the meditation.

The propagator of the *Yog Darśhan*, Maharshi Patanjali, states: *sthira sukhamāsanam* (2.46). 'To practise meditation sit motionless in any posture that you find comfortable.'

No matter what posture we adopt, we should sit alert. In sadhana, there is a tendency to become lazy and doze off to sleep. It happens because initially the material mind does not relish divine contemplation. When made to focus upon God, it becomes languid. Hence, we see people falling asleep during meditation and japa. To avoid this, it is important to sit upright during meditation.

The *Brahma Sūtra* (*Vedānt Darśhan*) has three aphorisms on the topic of sadhana:

āsīnah saṁbhavāt (4.1.7)

'To do sadhana, seat yourself properly.'

achalatvaṁ chāpekṣhya (4.1.9)

'Ensure that you sit upright and still.'

dhyānāchcha (4.1.8)

'Seated in this manner, focus the mind in meditation.'

Some people are unable to sit on the floor due to knee problems or joint pains. They need not feel discouraged; they can practise meditation while seated on a chair.

Q) What direction should we face while sitting in sadhana?

A) There is no restriction on direction. In Bhakti meditation, the aim is to purify the mind and rid it of material defects by absorbing it in the Supreme Divine Personality. He is all-pervading, so every direction is pure. The Vedic scriptures repeatedly propound the principle of the all-pervasiveness of God:

eko devaḥ sarvabhūteṣhu gūḍhaḥ sarvavyāpī
(*Śhwetāśhvatar Upaniṣhad* 6.11)

'There is one God. He is seated in everyone's heart. He is also everywhere in the world.'

puruṣha evedaṁ sarvaṁ yad bhūtaṁ yachcha bhāvyam
(*Puruṣh Sūktam* verse 2)

'God pervades everything that has existed and all that will exist.'

Hence, there is no need to make much ado of proper or improper direction. Instead, we should focus on the important point, which is the adornment of our inner thoughts with sublime sentiments.

Q) What or whom should we meditate upon?

A) A variety of meditation techniques exist in the world. There are Zen techniques, Buddhist techniques, Tantric techniques, and Taoist techniques among others. Each of these has many sub-branches and sub-sub-branches. Among the followers of Hinduism also, innumerable techniques of meditation are practised.

In deciding what to meditate upon, bear in mind that the aim of meditation is not merely to enhance concentration and focus, but also to purify the mind. Meditating on the breath, chakras, void, flame, and so on, is helpful in developing focus. However, purification of the mind is only effectively achieved when we fix it upon an all-pure entity, who is God Himself. This is the Bhakti Yog style of meditation, or Roop Dhyan that we discussed in the previous chapter on the power of visualisation. The Bhagavad Gita states:

māṁ cha yo 'vyabhichāreṇa bhakti-yogena sevate
sa guṇān samatītyaitān brahma-bhūyāya kalpate (14.26)

'Those who serve Me with unalloyed devotion rise above the three modes of material nature and come to the level of transcendence.'

According to the Vedas, the material energy consists of three *guṇas* (modes)—sattva (goodness), rajas (passion), and tamas (ignorance). These are referred to as the three modes of material nature. Everything made from material energy is within the realm of these three guṇas. Meditating upon the prana (life airs) may be called transcendental by its practitioners, but this is an inaccurate statement. True transcendental meditation is that where the object of meditation is God, who is beyond the modes of material nature.

Hence, the bottom-line is that the object of our meditation should be none other than the Supreme Lord Himself.

Integrating Contemplation, Meditation and Devotion in Our Sadhana

Having broadly discussed the various facets of sadhana, we can now get into the nitty-gritty of it. I have outlined here the different practical techniques we can incorporate in our sadhana.

Steps in Sadhana:

1) Make an altar with the images of God and guru and sit before it. This will help create the external environment

conducive for devotional absorption. Bear in mind that this step is not essential. Should you wish to meditate without external props, you can do that as well. For example, you may choose to sit up on your bed first thing after waking up and begin your meditation right away.

2) Sit in any comfortable pose. This was explained in detail in the previous section: *Common Questions on the Practice of Sadhana.*
3) Begin the sadhana by bringing God's image before you.

After step three, with the form of God in front, you can now practise any or all the methods of sadhana described here. These techniques are so powerful that each of them has the capacity to transform your mind from its core. Here is a quick recap of these practices which have been discussed in detail in previous chapters.

Spiritual Practice 1

Do Roop Dhyan meditation. You may visualise any image of God and/or guru in your heart or in front of you. This will give the mind a tangible basis to rest on. The detailed process of Roop Dhyan meditation has been described in chapter 9: *Visualisation and Roop Dhyan Meditation,* in the section: *Using Visualisation to Nurture Devotion.*

Spiritual Practice 2

Contemplate upon the wonderful divine virtues of God. This will help enchant your mind towards the Lord. The detailed process has been described in chapter 9: *Visualisation and Roop Dhyan Meditation,* in the section: *Meditation Upon Divine Qualities.*

Spiritual Practice 3

Repeatedly think about your eternal relationship with God, deepening your love for Him. Think: 'He is mine and I am His.' For a detailed explanation, read chapter 8: *Positive Self-Talk and Affirmation*, in the section: *Using Self-Talk to Programme Our Mind.*

Spiritual Practice 4

Through self-talk, train your mind in the spirit of surrender, as explained in chapter 6: *Getting Support of God's Grace*, in the section: *The Six Aspects of Surrender*. For example, repeatedly think: 'I must align my desire with God's desire. I must not desire anything against His will.'

Spiritual Practice 5

Cultivate selfless love by serving God in the mind. Such service will make you contemplate upon His happiness instead of your own. It will make you focus on giving rather than receiving. This was explained in chapter 9: *Visualisation and Roop Dhyan Meditation*, in the section: *Serving God in the Mind.*

Spiritual Practice 6

Take any gem of wisdom you found in this book and internalise it through the processes of śhravaṇ, manan, and nididhyāsan. This was elaborately explained in chapter 5: *Three Steps to Empower the Intellect.*

Spiritual Practice 7

Pray to God with complete sincerity of heart, shed tears of devotion, and beg Him for His grace. The goal is to develop an intense longing for the Lord while practising utmost humility. This has been described in chapter 9: *Visualisation and Roop Dhyan Meditation*, in the last section: *Meditation in the Sentiment of Longing.*

Spiritual Practice 8

After doing your daily sadhana, as described in the section above, for the rest of the day, practise the presence of God. This will help you do your worldly duties together with devotional remembrance of God. The detailed process was described in chapter 7: *Karm Yog for Everyday Living*, in the section: *Practice of the Presence of God.*

Any or all of these wonderful techniques mentioned above can be practised, either individually or in combinations, as a part of your daily spiritual practice.

Although these methods are straightforward and simple, yet beginners could find them daunting. What if someone is looking for an even simpler solution? There definitely is, and this is the process of kirtan (chanting).

The Popular Process of Chanting Kirtans

To simplify the sadhana and enable its practice in congregations, great saints in history composed kirtans. These are poetic verses filled with prayers, meditations, and sentiments of devotion. They are variously called hymns, *shabad*, or carols, in different religious traditions. These kirtans are filled with material for contemplation and reflection. When devotees hear and chant kirtans, they naturally internalise the *bhāv* (sentiments). Thus, through kirtans, people get an easy way to practise mind management.

What is the meaning of kirtan? Technically, it is defined as:

nāma-līlā-guṇadīnām uchchair-bhāṣhā tu kīrtanam
(*Bhakti Rasāmṛit Sindhu* 1.2.145)

'Singing the Names, Forms, Qualities, Pastimes, Abodes, and Associates of God is called kirtan.' It involves a three-fold process of devotion (*Tridhā Bhakti*), consisting of:

1) śhravaṇ (hearing)
2) kirtan (chanting)
3) smaraṇ (remembering)

The goal is to keep the mind focused upon God, and when done together with hearing and chanting, it becomes easier. The mind is as restless as the wind and naturally rambles from thought to thought. Hearing and chanting engage the senses, and this helps to repeatedly bring back the mind from its wanderings. Thus, kirtan is one of the most powerful means of practising devotion.

Kirtan has been the most popular form of devotion among saints in Indian history. All the famous bhakti saints—Soordas, Tulsidas, Meerabai, Guru Nanak, Kabir, Tukaram, Ekanath, Narsi Mehta, Jayadev, Tyagaraja, and others—were great poets. They composed numerous devotional songs and used them to engage in hearing, chanting, and remembering. The Vedic scriptures have also greatly extolled the virtues of kirtan:

kalerdoṣha nidherājannastihyeko mahān guṇaḥ
kīrtanād eva kṛiṣhṇasya muktasaṅgaḥ paraṁ vrajet
(Shreemad Bhagavatam 12.3.51).

'*Kaliyug* is an ocean of faults, but it has one great quality. By doing kirtan of Shree Krishna, one is easily liberated from maya and attains the divine Abode.'

avikārī vā vikārī vā sarva doṣhaika bhājanaḥ
parameśha padaṁ yāti rāma nāmānukīrtanāt

(*Adhyātma Rāmāyaṇ*)

'Whether one is without desires or full of desires, faultless or full of faults, if one chants the Names of Shree Ram, one will attain God-realisation.'

pāpānalasya dīptasya mā kurvantu bhayaṁ narāḥ
govinda nāma meghaughairnaśhyate nīra bindubhiḥ

(*Garuḍ Purāṇ*)

'Humans should not worry about the burning fire of past sins; the raindrops from the clouds of God's Holy Name will extinguish it easily.'

harernāma harernāma harernāmaiva kevalam
kalau nāstyeva nāstyeva nāstyeva gatiranyathā

(*Bṛihan Nāradīya Purāṇa*)

'Declare it three times that the name of God is my very life. In *Kaliyug* there is no other means for salvation. no other means, no other means.'

ehiñ kalikāla na sādhana dūjā,
yoga yagya japa tapa vrata pūjā
rāmahi sumiria gāia rāmahi,
santata sunia rāma guna grāmahi (Ramayan)

'In this age of Kali, no other spiritual practice is successful—neither Ashtang Yog, fire sacrifice, chanting on the rosary, austerities, or fasts. Simply sing the glories of Ram, hear them from the saints, and remember them in the mind.'

Thus, we see how the Vedic scriptures have unanimously praised the importance and benefits of kirtan. Still, we must not forget that mechanical chanting by itself will not purify the mind. Hearing and chanting are only helpers while the essence is remembrance. Always keeping the mind attached to God is of paramount importance.

KripaluPadhati

Earlier in this chapter, eight spiritual practices were enlisted for integrating in our daily practice of sadhana. This can be a daunting task for most aspirants. It is often wiser for the teacher to provide a simple solution—a template that the student can latch onto for support. With that in mind, I have prepared the **KripaluPadhati**, which is a simple template for sadhana incorporating the principles explained in this book.

One-hour format for sadhana:

20 minutes – Listen to a lecture
10 minutes – Roop Dhyan meditation
5 minutes – Daily prayer
20 minutes – Kirtan (chanting meditation)
5 minutes – *Ārati* (ceremony of lights)

----

60 minutes – Total duration

The Daily Sadhana Online Platform

If you like this 60-minute format for your spiritual practice, you can try the online portal my team has created at *www.mydailysadhana.org*. It is a unique spiritual platform for seekers of all backgrounds to make regular spiritual progress at their own pace and in the comfort of their own home. Through it, you can practise spirituality every day in a structured and engaging manner.

Daily sadhana will help you to learn and imbibe the timeless Vedic philosophy through carefully designed courses that have been systematically organised into daily lessons.

- Each daily lesson is comprised of an exclusive lecture, review slides, audio narrations, quizzes, and exercises to help test your understanding and measure your progress.
- Practise what you learn every day through exclusive guided meditations and kirtan sessions.
- Participate in interactive forums where you can submit questions and get answers from the daily sadhana community.
- Accumulate bonus points by completing daily tasks and redeem them for books, cds, dvds, and exclusive audio-video downloads.

Daily sadhana is completely mobile friendly and can e accessed through multiple platforms. Visit *www.nydailysadhana.org* for more information and to enrol.

Repeated Practice Leads to Perfection

We all know the axiom: 'Practice makes perfect.' This is even more applicable in the field of spiritual sadhana, for the harsh reality is that the mind is restless, turbulent, strong, and obstinate.

- The mind is restless because it keeps flitting in different directions from subject to subject.
- It is turbulent because it creates upheavals in one's consciousness, in the form of hatred, anger, greed, and attachment.
- It is strong because it overpowers the intellect with its vigorous currents and destroys the faculty of discernment.
- It is also obstinate because when it catches a harmful thought, it refuses to let go, and continues to ruminate over it again and again even to the dismay of the intellect.

Thus, when we begin practising the techniques described in the previous sections, we will encounter a serious obstacle. We will experience that no matter how hard we try to focus the mind, it comes away from the divine and returns to the material.

In the Bhagavad Gita, verse 6.34, Arjun confessed this problem to the Lord:

chañchalaṁ hi manaḥ kṛiṣhṇa pramāthi balavad dṛiḍham
tasyāhaṁ nigrahaṁ manye vāyor iva su-duṣhkaram

He told Shree Krishna that he finds the mind even more difficult to control than the wind. It was a powerful analogy for no one can ever think of controlling the mighty wind in the sky.

Lord Krishna did not deny the problem. For instance, he could have downplayed it by saying, 'Arjun, what rubbish are you talking? The mind can be controlled very easily.' Rather, He concurred that the mind is indeed difficult to control. But difficult does not mean impossible. Many things are difficult to achieve in the world and yet we are not discouraged to strive for them.

For example, sailors know that the sea is dangerous, and the possibility of terrible storms exists. Yet, they have never found these dangers as sufficient reasons for remaining ashore. Motorists know that accidents happen on highways and yet they take the risk of driving many hours every day.

Lord Krishna responded to Arjun's comment by calling him *Mahābāho,* meaning 'Mighty armed one':

asanśhayaṁ mahā-bāho mano durnigrahaṁ chalam
abhyāsena tu kaunteya vairāgyeṇa cha gṛihyate

(Bhagavad Gita 6.35)

He implied, 'O Arjun, you defeated the bravest warriors in battle. Can you not defeat the mind?' He assured Arjun that the mind can be controlled but it requires the twin remedies of *vairāgya* and *abhyās*. Vairāgya means detachment from the material world. It prevents the mind from running in the direction of its attachment, towards the objects it has been habituated to desiring in the past. Abhyās means practice or a concerted and persistent effort to change an old habit to develop a new one.

Practice is thus the essential factor for mind management. In fact, in all fields of human endeavour, practice is the key that opens the door to mastery and excellence. Similarly, the obstinate and turbulent mind has to be made to rest at the lotus feet of the Supreme Lord through abhyās.

Maharshi Patanjali has given the same instruction in his aphorisms: *abhyāsa vairāgyābhyāṁ tannirodhaḥ* (*Yog Darśhan* 1.12). 'The perturbations of the mind can be controlled by constant practice and detachment.' Take the mind away from the world—this is vairāgya—and bring the mind to rest on God—this is abhyās.

We now discuss a simple technique to bring the mind back to God in case it wanders away.

Wherever the Mind Wanders, Realise God There

How can a monkey be trained? It is undoubtedly a restless creature and yet monkey tamers train it to the point where they make it sit peacefully and perform tricks when asked. What is the secret by which it gets disciplined?

On the first day, the trainer ties the monkey with a hundred-foot rope and lets it play. When the monkey attempts to run beyond its periphery, the rope tugs at its neck. Then it understands that it is preferable to jump and play within the hundred feet circle. The next day, the trainer shortens the rope to fifty feet. Again, the monkey attempts to go beyond, but the rope constrains it, and it learns to remain in the smaller boundary. In this way, when the rope becomes only six feet, the monkey decides that jumping is no fun, and it might as well sit still.

Our mind too is restless like the monkey and seeks to flit from object to object. But if we can learn to yoke it to the rope of the Lord, it soon becomes subdued.

What does it mean to yoke the mind to God? Let us say that you begin your meditation by bringing the image of Lord Krishna before you. However, in a few moments, you find that God's image has vanished, and your mind now holds onto your spouse's image. When this happens, people become agitated. But this only worsens the situation. If you scold your mind, 'I have told you so many times to think of God, and yet you come away,' then the mind loses even its remaining poise and serenity. **Instead, wherever the mind wanders, therein realise the presence of God.** In this way, the mind will again get diverted to Him.

For example, if your mind wandered to your spouse's attractive eyes, realise the presence of Lord Krishna there, and think, 'Shree Krishna is sitting in my spouse's eyes and saying, "Look it is I who am the basis of beauty anywhere. If you are enticed by beauty, seek it in My divine form, which is infinitely more gorgeous."' The idea is to think in a manner that somehow keeps the mind yoked to God. The Bhagavad Gita states:

yo māṁ paśhyati sarvatra sarvaṁ cha mayi paśhyati
tasyāhaṁ na praṇaśhyāmi sa cha me na praṇaśhyati (6.30)

'For those who see Me everywhere and see all things in Me, I am never lost, nor are they ever lost to Me.' In this verse, to lose God means to let the mind wander away from Him, and to be with Him means to unite the mind with Him.

As another example, let us say that someone hurts us. Now, it is the nature of the mind to develop sentiments of resentment, hatred, and anger towards anyone who harms us. However, if we permit that to happen, then our mind will come away from the divine realm, and the devotional union of our mind with God will cease. Instead, if we see the Supreme Lord seated in that person, we will think, 'God is testing me through this person. He wants me to increase the virtue of tolerance, and that is why He is inspiring this person to behave badly with me. But I will not permit the incident to disturb me.' Thinking in this way, we will be able to prevent the mind from becoming a victim of negative sentiments.

Similarly, the mind disconnects from God when it gets attached to a friend or relative. Instead, if we train the mind to see God in that person, then each time the mind wanders towards him or her, we will think, 'Shree Krishna is seated in this person, and thus I am feeling this attraction.' In this manner, the mind will continue to retain its devotional absorption in the Supreme Lord.

Sometimes, the mind ponders over past incidents. Lamentation takes the mind into the past, and consequently, the present remembrance of God ceases. Instead, if we see the past incident in connection with God, we could think, 'The Lord deliberately arranged for me to experience tribulation, so that I may develop detachment from worldly things and turn towards Him. He is so concerned about my welfare that He mercifully sends circumstances beneficial for my spiritual progress.' By thinking thus, we protect our devotional absorption.

The *Nārad Bhakti Darśhan* states: *loka hānau chintā na kāryā niveditātma loka vedatvāt* (*Sūtra* 61): 'When you suffer a reversal in the world, do not lament about it. See the grace of God in that incident.'

Our self-interest lies in somehow or the other keeping the mind in God, and the simple trick to accomplish this is to see God in everything and everyone. This practice slowly leads to perfection where the mind learns to be always united with God.

In Conclusion

God has placed this immensely powerful mind at our disposal. Every machine we purchase comes with a user manual that enables us to figure out its working. We came into the world fitted with the wonderful machine called the mind. What we direly need is a user manual on its workings. Without such a guide, unravelling the mysteries of the mind becomes a daunting task. This book was written to serve as your reference guide for the mind.

You must now lift the internal armaments of mind management that you have studied in this book and courageously vanquish the enemies from within. The inner battle is never an easy one, but it is the most important battle in life. Every victory will open doors to immense treasures of the soul and the divine treasures that exist within you. May the blessings of the Supreme Lord be upon you for all success in your efforts!

SUMMARY OF THE MAIN POINTS

Implementation of spiritual knowledge requires sadhana.

We must firmly resolve to dedicate at least an hour every day to sadhana. This will help u s maintain divine consciousness during the rest of the day as well.

- Sadhana should be practised in an environment of seclusion, with minimal worldly distractions, as this is conducive to absorbing the mind in divine thoughts.
- For sadhana, sit in any comfortable posture, Begin the sadhana by bringing God's image before you.
- Contemplate upon His wonderful divine qualities. Repeatedly thinks about your eternal relationship with Him. Practice selfless love by serving God n the mind.
- Take any piece of knowledge, an d go through the processes of shravan, manan, and nididhyasan.
- Train your mind in the spirit of surrender through self-talk.
- Pray to God with all the sincerity of your heart, shedding tears of devotion, and begging Him for His grace.
- As an aid in your sadhana, chant a kirtan containing any or all of the following: a prayer, a meditation, a contemplation, sentiments of introspections, or simply the Name of God.
- Do not be discouraged when the mind wanders away. Bring it back by detachment and practice. Wherever the mind goes, practise to realise there the presence of God

GLOSSARY

Ārati	a hymn which is all about the glories of God
Abhyāṣ	practice
Ahankār	ego
Ahimsa	non-violence
Annamaya kośh	one of the five sheaths surrounding the soul. This is the physical body and the outermost sheath
Antaḥ karaṇ	mind or ethereal heart
Apauruṣheya	not created by any human
Asan	posture, can be sitting or standing
Bahisht	heaven (in Arabic)
Bhajan	hymn
Bhakti	love for God
Bhāv	sentiments
Buddhi	intellect
Buddhi Yog	yoga of the intellect
Chintan	repetition of a thought, idea, or piece of knowledge, in the mind and intellect

Chitta	subconscious mind
Darśhan	vision of God
Doṣhaj	diseases that come as reactions to bad karmas from our past lives
Dozakh	hell (in Arabic)
God-realisation	union of our soul with the Supreme Soul
Gopis	the maidens of the land of Braj where Radha Krishna descended and performed various leelas
Gulab jamun	an Indian dessert made from milk solids (khoya). The milk solids are kneaded into a dough from which little balls are made, deep-fried, and immersed in sugar syrup
Guṇas	the three modes of material nature
Guru	the enlightened spiritual teacher who is our guide and mentor on the spiritual path
Jagadguru	guru of the entire world
Jagadguruttam	supreme amongst all Jagadgurus
Jalebi	an Indian dessert made by deep frying flour batter in circles. The fried circles are then soaked in sugar syrup
Japa	the chanting of the Names of God
Jīvātmā	soul

Kām	lust
Kāmanā	desire
Karm yog	as explained in the Bhagavad Gita, the practice of keeping the mind attached to the Divine at all times while performing our everyday tasks
Karm yogi	one who performs worldly duties with the body, while the mind is attached to God
Karma	past actions, either in previous lifetimes or in the current life
Karmaj	diseases that are a consequence of unhealthy habits and lifestyle in the present life
Kārnāmās	actions (in Arabic)
Kayāmat	day of reckoning (in Arabic)
Kesar	saffron
Kheer	Indian rice pudding
Kirtan	hearing, singing, and remembering the Names, Forms, Qualities, Pastimes, Abodes, and Associates of God
Leelas	pastimes of the Divine
Mana	mind
Manan	contemplation upon the divine knowledge
Mānas rog	mental illnesses

Manasī sevā	service in the mind, by thought
Manomaya kośh	one of the five sheaths surrounding the soul. This is the mental sheath and the third sheath from the inside out
Maya	God's material energy
Mṛiga tṛishṇā	a mirage
Nididhyāsan	process of consciously forming beliefs based on the knowledge from the scriptures
Pada	hymn
Pandit	Indian priest
Placebo effect	See Remembered Wellness
Pooja	to worship God, God-realised saints, or highly elevated personalities
Prāṇ	life airs
Prāṇamaya kośh	one of the five sheaths surrounding the soul. This is the vital energy sheath and the fourth sheath from the inside out
Preya	pleasure which seems pleasant in the beginning, but causes great pain later
Remembered Illness	a psychosomatic state where the mind recalls previous instances of the body's illness and starts experiencing those symptoms again without any external cause or trigger

Remembered Wellness	a psychosomatic state where the mind recalls previous instances of the body's wellness and the body responds accordingly
Rajas	mode of passion
Rasgulla	Indian dessert made from cottage cheese (chenna) and immersed in sugar syrup
Roop Dhyān	a meditation technique propagated by Jagadguru Kripalu-ji Maharaj in which the meditator sits with eyes closed and focuses on an image or images of any form of God
Sadhana	spiritual practice, usually done daily
sankalp	to desire something or someone; to hanker for; to long for
Sanskārs	accumulated tendencies from endless (previous) lifetimes
Satsang	devotional gathering
Sattva	mode of goodness
Śatya	truthfulness
Sevā	service to God
Shakti	energy
Śharaṇāgati	surrender of the mind, intellect, and ego to God
Śhāstras	the Vedic scriptures
Śhravaṇ	process of hearing divine knowledge

Śhreya	pleasure which seems bitter in the beginning, but becomes very sweet in the long run
Śhruti	knowledge received by hearing
Smaraṇ	remembrance
Sudarśhan Chakra	divine disc in Lord Vishnu's hand
Tamas	mode of ignorance
Vairāgya	detachment from the material world
Viraha dhyān	meditation with the sentiment of longing to see a dear one
Viraha vedanā	an intense longing for God
Vivek	power of discernment such that the intellect rules the mind
Yajna	a fire sacrifice performed as a ritual, accompanied by the recitation of different mantras
Yog	union with God

GUIDE TO HINDI PRONUNCIATION

a	as *u* in b*u*t
ā	as *a* in f*a*r
i	as *i* in p*i*n
ī	as *i* in mach*i*ne
u	as *u* in p*u*sh
ū	as *o* in m*o*ve
e	as *a* in ev*a*de
ai	as *a* in m*a*t; sometimes as *ai* in *ai*sle with the only difference that *a* should be pronounced as *u* in b*u*t, not as *a* in f*a*r
o	as *o* in g*o*
au	as *o* in p*o*t, or as *aw* in s*aw*
ṛi	as *ri* in K*ri*shna
ḥ	it is a strong aspirate; also lengthens the preceding vowel and occurs only at the end of a word. It is pronounced as a final *h* sound

ṁ	nasalises and lengthens the preceding vowel and is pronounced as *n* in the French word Bo*n*.
ka	as *k* in *k*ite
kha	as *kh* in Ec*kh*art
ga	as *g* in *g*oat
gha	as *gh* in di*gh*ard
ṅ	as *n* in fi*n*ger
cha	as *ch* in *ch*anel
chha	as *chh* in staun*chh*eart
ja	as *j* in *j*ar
jha	as *dgeh* in he*dgeh*og
ñ	as *n* in lu*n*ch
ṭa	as *t* in *t*ub
ṭha	as *th* in ho*th*ead
ḍa	as *d* in *d*ivine
ḍha	as *dh* in re*dh*ead
ṇa	as *n* in bur*n*t
ta	as *t* in French word ma*t*ron
tha	as *th* in e*th*er
da	as *th* in ei*th*er
dha	as *dh* in Bud*dh*a
na	as *n* in *n*o
pa	as *p* in *p*ink
pha	as *ph* in u*ph*ill

ba	as *b* in *boy*
bha	as *bh* in a*bh*or
ma	as *m* in *m*an
ya	as *y* in *y*es
ra	as *r* in *r*emember
la	as *l* in *l*ight
va	as *v* in *v*ine, as *w* in s*w*an
śha	as *sh* in *sh*ape
sa	as *s* in *s*in
ṣha	as *sh* in *sh*ow
ha	as *h* in *h*ut
kṣha	as *ksh* in frea*ksh*ow
ña	as *gy* in bi*gy*oung
ṛa	There is no sign in English to represent the sound ड़. It has been written as *ṛa* but the tip of the tongue quickly flaps down.
ṛha	There is no sign in English to represent the sound ढ़. It has been written as *ṛha* but the tip of the tongue quickly flaps down.
ṛī	*as ree in* spree

Other Books by the Author

7 Mindsets for Success, Happiness, and Fulfilment

Bhagavad Gita, The Song of God

Essence of Hinduism

Science of Healthy Diet

Spiritual Dialectics

Yoga for Mind, Body, and Soul

Books for Children

Bal-Mukund Wisdom Book

Festivals of India

Healthy Body, Healthy Mind: Yoga for Children

Inspiring Stories for Children (set of 4 books)

Mahabharat

My Best Friend Krishna

Ramayana

Saints of India

Let's Connect

If you enjoyed reading this book and would like to connect with Swami Mukundananda, you can reach him through any of the following channels:

Websites: www.jkyog.org, www.jkyog.in

YouTube channels: 'Swami Mukundananda' and 'Swami Mukundananda Hindi'

Facebook: 'Swami Mukundananda' and 'Swami Mukundananda Hindi'

Instagram: 'Swami Mukundananda' and 'Swami Mukundananda Hindi'

Twitter: Swami Mukundananda (@Sw_Mukundananda)

LinkedIn: Swami Mukundananda

Podcasts: Apple, Google, SoundCloud, Spotify, Stitcher

JKYog Radio: TuneIn app for iOS (Apple App Store) and Android (Google Play Store)

JKYog App: Available for iOS (Apple App Store) and Android (Google Play Store)

WhatsApp Daily Inspirations: We have two broadcast lists. You are welcome to join either or both.

USA: +1 346-239-9675

India: +91 84489 41008

Email: deskofswamiji@swamimukundananda.org

To bring *Science of Mind Management* or Swami Mukundananda to your organisation—as Google, Intel, Oracle, Verizon, United Nations, Stanford University, Yale University, IITs and IIMs have—please write to deskofswamiji@swamimukundananda.org